John Fletcher Hurst

Short History of the Church in the United States, A.D. 1492-1890

John Fletcher Hurst

Short History of the Church in the United States, A.D. 1492-1890

ISBN/EAN: 9783337003111

Printed in Europe, USA, Canada, Australia, Japan

Cover: Foto ©ninafisch / pixelio.de

More available books at **www.hansebooks.com**

SHORT HISTORY

OF THE

CHURCH IN THE UNITED STATES

A.D. 1492–1890

BY

JOHN F. HURST, D.D.

AUTHOR OF "SHORT HISTORY OF THE EARLY CHURCH"
"SHORT HISTORY OF THE MODERN CHURCH IN EUROPE"
"SHORT HISTORY OF THE REFORMATION" ETC.

NEW YORK
CHAUTAUQUA PRESS
C. L. S. C. DEPARTMENT
150 FIFTH AVENUE
1890

The required books of the C. L. S. C. are recommended by a Council of six. It must, however, be understood that recommendation does not involve an approval by the Council, or by any member of it, of every principle or doctrine contained in the book recommended.

CONTENTS.

PART I.—THE COLONIAL PERIOD.

CHAPTER	PAGE
I. THE NEW CHRISTENDOM	1
II. THE SPANISH COLONIZATION	4
III. THE FRENCH COLONIZATION	8
IV. THE ENGLISH COLONIZATION: VIRGINIA AND MASSACHUSETTS	12
V. MARYLAND, PENNSYLVANIA, AND OTHER ENGLISH COLONIES	17
VI. CONTINENTAL COLONIES: DUTCH, SWEDES, HUGUENOTS, AND OTHER PROTESTANTS	21
VII. THE PROVIDENTIAL PLANTING	25
VIII. POLITICAL FRAMEWORK OF THE COLONIES.	28
IX. CHURCH GOVERNMENT IN THE COLONIES	31
X. EDUCATION	35
XI. INTOLERANCE IN THE COLONIES.	40
XII. RELIGIOUS LIFE OF THE COLONIES.	46
XIII. COLONIAL WORSHIP AND USAGES	49
XIV. MISSIONS TO THE INDIANS.	52
XV. THEOLOGICAL MOVEMENTS.	57

PART II.—THE NATIONAL PERIOD.

CHAPTER	PAGE
I. The Church at the Founding of the Republic	62
II. The Separation of Church and State	65
III. The Revival at the Beginning of the Century	67
IV. Expansion in the South and West	69
V. The Large and Earlier Denominations	72
VI. The Smaller Evangelical Bodies	78
VII. The Quakers	81
VIII. The Roman Catholic Church	82
IX. The Unitarian Church	85
X. The Transcendentalists	87
XI. Universalists and other Smaller Bodies	89
XII. The Mormon Abomination	92
XIII. The Anti-slavery Reform	95
XIV. The Temperance Reform	99
XV. Philanthropy and Christian Union	103
XVI. Missions	107
XVII. Christian Literature	111
XVIII. The Sunday-school	117
XIX. The American Pulpit	120
XX. Theology of the American Church	123
INDEX	127

SHORT HISTORY

OF THE

CHURCH IN THE UNITED STATES.

I.

The Colonial Period.
1492–1783.

Chapter I.

THE NEW CHRISTENDOM.

1. **Europe in the Sixteenth Century** was in convulsion. The Reformation had already stirred England to its centre by the fearless labors of Wyclif, while Huss of Bohemia had uttered a cry of warning which was heard throughout the Continent and awakened fear in Rome. These reformatory movements reacted on the political life of all the central nations. Not a throne was safe where the new religious revolt was in full force. The entire sixteenth century was a period of universal disturbance. The progress of reform provoked violent hostility, and every land was divided into factions. There were three general grades of sentiment. One class, receiving its inspiration from Rome, wished to continue the old order, with the Pope as practical sovereign. Another class, craving liberty and an ac-

commodation to the new order, was willing to break loose from the Roman see, but desired to retain many of the Romish usages. The third class saw nothing but antichrist in Rome, and found hope only in casting off every reminder of papal doctrine and custom.

2. **The Transferal of European Conflicts** to America was the new order. Whenever a colony came to America, it no sooner settled in its new habitat than it revived, under broader conditions, the struggle in which it had been engaged in Europe. The cavalier of the Virginia Colony surrendered none of his old attachment to the Church of England. The Plymouth Pilgrim was even more intense in his revolt against both Romanism and Protestant Episcopacy than he had been when he was a Brownist at Scrooby, a parishioner of Robinson in Leyden, or a Pilgrim on the *Mayflower*. In the new world were fought out, in smaller numbers, and by contestants more dispersed, the issues which had driven the colonists to the Western wilds.

3. **The Religious Motive** was supreme in the mind of all the best colonists. To enjoy the free exercise of conscience was the Pilgrim's one passion, whose bright flame no distance from native land, nor stormy seas, nor rigor of climate, nor danger of death by savage hands could quench. Our first settlers came as Christians, lived as Christians, and planted the religious principle as the richest inheritance for their posterity. The Pilgrims, before leaving England, had no thought of separating from the Established Church, but longed for reformation within it; and they resolved on the expedient of emigration only when James I. deceived them, and said: "I will make them conform or harry them out of the land." "The charter of the first colony," says Baird, "that of Virginia, provided that the

whole settlement should have a Christian character, and enjoined the worship of the Church of England, requiring every male colonist of sixteen and upward to pay ten pounds of tobacco and one bushel of corn for the support of the Church. When the Puritans gained ascendency in England, under the Protectorate of Cromwell, Virginia and the Carolinas became the refuge for the Cavalier and the Churchman, as afterwards of the Huguenot and the German Protestant. Georgia was colonized expressly as an asylum for imprisoned and persecuted Bohemians and the inhabitants of the Italian valleys, and the Colony of Gustavus Adolphus was to be a blessing to the whole Protestant world by offering a shelter to all who stood in need of one."

Chapter II.

THE SPANISH COLONIZATION.

1. **The Earliest on the New American field** were the Spanish discoverers and conquerors. When Columbus discovered the little West India island of San Salvador, and raised upon the shore the cross, he dedicated it and the lands beyond to his sovereigns, Ferdinand and Isabella. The "Gloria in Excelsis" was sung by the discoverer and his weary crew with as much fervor as it had ever been chanted in the cathedrals of Spain. The faith was the Roman Catholic. On his second voyage, in 1494, Columbus took with him a vicar apostolic and twelve priests, and on the island of Hayti erected the first chapel in the Western World. The success of Columbus in discovering a new world in the west awakened a wild enthusiasm throughout Europe. Visions of gold inflamed the minds alike of rulers, knights, and adventurers. To discover and gather treasures, and organize vast missionary undertakings, became the mania of the times. No European country which possessed a strip of seaboard escaped the delirium. To send out a vessel or a fleet to the new world was the fashion of the palace and the capitalist.

2. **Mexico** was the first broad field of conquest by the Spaniards. Cortes led the expedition, and in 1520 landed at a point which still bears the name of Vera Cruz (the True Cross). He conciliated a tribe which was in rebellion against the Aztec king Montezuma,

and succeeded in dethroning the king, and bringing the country into subjection to Spain. The colonists, who arrived in quick succession, had among their members earnest priests, to whom it was a passion to carry the cross into the interior, and to convert, by any means, the aborigines to the Gospel of Christ. From the capital, Mexico, missionaries representing the principal Roman orders penetrated all parts of the new province, reached the shores of the Pacific, and formed a line of missions up the Pacific nearly to the present state of Washington.

3. **Other fields**, more or less dependent on Mexico, were rapidly added to the Spanish domain in America. In 1542 Coronado led an expedition northward into the New Mexico and Arizona of our day, and the mission of the priest continued after that of the military adventurer was ended. The traces of this expedition are still to be seen in the old churches of Santa Fé and Tucson, and in the Roman Catholic faith of the mixed Indian and Spanish population. The conquest of Florida was begun by Pamphilo de Narvaez in 1526, and completed about 1601. A Huguenot colony was established there, but the Spaniards would not allow it to live. They murdered the Huguenots, and established their own missions on the spot. Texas was organized into a mission by Father de Olmos in 1546. De Soto explored the Mississippi Valley. Vasco Nuñez de Balboa and Alonzo de Ojeda explored the Isthmus of Darien, and added the contiguous regions to the same broadening domain of Spain and the Roman communion.

4. **The Evils of Spanish Colonization** were manifested in each of these sections. The conqueror was devoted to the Church, and missionaries became willing tools

to compel obedience to the new Spanish authority. Wherever the natives refused allegiance to the religion of the conquerors, they were persecuted and even put to death. Las Casas, the one humane servant of his Church, reports that in Yucatan alone five millions of Mexican aborigines were slaughtered. The curse of Spanish cruelty in Mexico has never been counterbalanced by beneficence in other departments. The Aztec and other native races have always cherished a violent hostility to the very name of the Spaniard. As if a divine Nemesis had watched over those suffering people for three centuries, the freedom from Spanish rule and the birth of the Mexican Republic have been brought about by descendants of the natives whom the Spaniards persecuted. Juarez, the Washington of Mexico, was an Indian, and the first president, Diaz, is in part Indian, while Altamirano and other leading literary characters are of unmixed Indian blood.

5. All the Spanish Colonies in North America shared with Mexico the same narrow spirit. The Spaniard was in the New World to get what he could; to enforce his faith; to carry back gold to enrich the coffers of Spain and the Pope; to add to his own dignity by grinding down the conquered races. Florida, the Mississippi Valley, the Pacific Coast, the West India Islands, and Central America became a vast feudatory territory, whose treasures were used for filling foreign coffers, and whose people were regarded as little better than slaves.

6. Scanty Education was imparted to these millions newly added to the Roman faith. Some of the priests translated devotional and doctrinal treatises into the native tongues, in order the better to reach the people. The printing-press was early erected in both Mexico

THE SPANISH COLONIZATION. 7

and Vera Cruz, but only as an instrument of ecclesiastical authority. Molina published in Mexico an Aztec and Spanish Dictionary in 1545—the first important philological work printed in America. Small works by Zumaraga were also published in the Aztec tongue in the city of Mexico. Many devotional works in the Spanish language were printed in Spain and Flanders, and introduced into Mexico for the better holding of the increasing Spanish population in willing subjection to the Roman Catholic Church.

Chapter III.

THE FRENCH COLONIZATION.

1. France Looking Westward.—Very soon after the discovery of America the French mariners caught from Spain and Portugal the spirit of discovery, and went westward in search of new lands, to add them to the dominion of France. They explored the regions of the present dominion of Canada, which became known on the map of the world as New France. They threaded the Mississippi, and planted colonies at favorable points. They formed friendly relations with the Indian tribes, and built up a powerful system of colonies, half religious and half political, which grew in strength as time advanced. This was the French Roman Catholic current to America, which, later, threatened to extinguish the Anglo-Saxon domination.

2. The French Navigators who came to the Western World were prompted by the spirit of discovery, financial gain, and temporal dominion. They were not willing that the Spanish, Portuguese, and English should monopolize either the glory or the advantage of discoveries and colonization on the continent. Verrezano led an expedition in 1524 to North Carolina, and went northward as far as Newfoundland. Cartier continued where Verrezano left off, explored the Gulf of St. Lawrence, ascended the river as far as where Montreal now stands, and penetrated the great wilds of Canada. Champlain made still further explorations. He founded Quebec, and, in 1608, made it the centre of his authority in New France. He entered into friendly relations with the great Indian tribes. Under him the authority of France was established, and a new and vast territory was added to the domains of the French king.

3. **The French along the Great Lakes.**—The French had only to continue their exploration westward. No European colony stood in their way. Their Jesuit missionaries, who accompanied every exploring expedition, organized missions, taught the elements of their doctrines to the new Indian members, and counted no sacrifice too dear to convert the savages to Christianity. Montreal was founded, and became the seat of a strong Jesuit missionary force. Detroit was added to the map of the Jesuit world. The Huron tribes, whose northern territory skirted the frozen zone, became a special object of Jesuit zeal. So intense was this new enthusiasm that the northern regions of the present states of Maine and New York became a mission field. Here labored Fathers Druellettes and Jogues, who exhibited all the energy of Xavier in braving dangers from savages and the elements. On both sides of the St. Lawrence, and striking far into the interior, and going ever westward, the chain of missions extended along the shores of Lake Michigan, and to the far-off region of Lake Superior. Rome and France divided the glory. Realistic accounts were sent back to Europe, and an intense sympathy was aroused, in palace and hut, in behalf of the evangelization of tribes whose existence the Jesuit missionaries were the first to make known to the European world.

4. **The Mississippi Valley** was explored by the French, and wherever the explorers went the Jesuit fathers established missions. Joliet, the layman, and Father

Marquette, the Jesuit priest, continued westward until they struck the headwaters of the Mississippi, and descended it as far as the mouth of the Arkansas, when they returned to Canada. La Salle, more bold, descended the river to the Gulf of Mexico, and proclaimed the valley of the Mississippi a possession of his king, Louis XIV. of France. Iberville sailed from France in 1698 with an expedition, and later, in 1700, established a French colony near the mouth of the Mississippi. In the path of these explorations missions were established at every convenient point. Indians were gathered into the Roman fold along the great river and its tributaries. A chain of missions extended from the gulf directly northward into the interior of Canada, and thence eastward as far as the Gulf of St. Lawrence and the Atlantic Ocean.

5. **The Outcome** of the great French colonial system, in its early period, promised largely. The leading Jesuit fathers were heroes in endurance and daring. In the annals of the Christian Church their self-sacrifice is not surpassed. The accounts which they sent back to France concerning their work, and which pass by the name of the "Jesuit Relations," are among the rarest and most brilliant narratives of missionary operations produced by the modern Church. As time advanced, the Jesuit character passed largely from the spiritual guide into the political agent. No European in America has ever possessed the confidence of the Indian as did the French Jesuit. While the first lesson which the western and the northern Indian was taught was loyalty to Christ, in the same breath was taught loyalty to the king of France. In time the second loyalty was the stronger lesson. The Indian was urged to hate the English. The Englishman was loathed as

the Protestant, and therefore the enemy. The colonial missions along the Mississippi now grew in commercial importance. The chain along the Lakes, extending from the northwestern limit of Lake Superior to the Atlantic Ocean, was far behind the English advance in New England, the middle, and the southern colonies. There was religious stagnation and political retrogression.

6. **English and French Colonists** in Canada had now developed so far, and had come into such frequent collision, that a final solution was soon to be reached. The struggle between the English on the one side and the French and Indians on the other, at Fort Duquesne, the present Pittsburgh, in 1754, resulted in the defeat of the English under Braddock. This gave the whole west into the hands of the French. But the English were not ready to surrender the contest. The war was carried into Canada and along the southern side of the St. Lawrence. Monckton subdued the French in Nova Scotia in 1755. Fort Duquesne, Frontenac, and Louisbourg fell into English hands in 1758. Niagara, Crown Point, and Ticonderoga were now also wrested from the French. The final struggle was for Quebec. Here the English also won. Wolfe received a fatal wound, but when told "They run!" he had strength to ask, "Who run?" The answer was, "The French." He answered, "I thank God; I die happy."

This was the end of French dominion in Canada. All the vast dreams of a New France in the Western World were now over. The treaty which followed the fall of Quebec gave all the territory east of the Mississippi to England. This conquest of Canada by the English was second only to the Revolutionary War in its effects on Protestantism in America. Without it, the success of the Revolution would hardly have been possible.

Chapter IV.

THE ENGLISH COLONIZATION: VIRGINIA AND MASSACHUSETTS.

1. The First English Discoveries.—England was profoundly impressed by the Spanish discoveries in America. Her rulers and her sailors were alike anxious, from different motives, to gather into the British domain whatever treasures and territory the New World might give them. It was a European race for gold, for furs, for land. So far, Spain had the advantage. But the Anglo-Saxon, in all modern history, has been the king of circumstance. Four years after Columbus knelt on the shore of the little island of San Salvador, and raised the cross, John Cabot sailed from England westward to reach China. Henry VII. gave him authority to discover unknown lands, and incorporate them with the British Isles. While he sailed for China, he touched the bleak shore of Labrador. On a second voyage he discovered Newfoundland and the New England coast, and skirted the Atlantic coast down to Florida. Other English discoverers followed in his bold ocean pathway—Martin Frobisher, Sir Humphrey Gilbert, Captain John Smith, Sir Walter Raleigh, and Gorges. Sir Humphrey Gilbert was lost at sea, and shortly before his death he was heard to say, "We are as near heaven by sea as by land." Wherever these discoverers went they laid claim to the land in the name of the British crown. It was little concern whether

Spain or France had already claimed it. The future would decide which was the abler to hold and colonize.

2. **The James River Colony.**—The first stage in development was to colonize. The James River Colony was the first attempt at permanent occupation. This colony consisted of English cavaliers, devoted adherents of the Established Church. The colonists arrived in Virginia, and settled on the bank of James River, in 1603. The easy-going, gentlemanly element predominated. Of the one hundred and five colonists, only twelve were tillers of the soil. The leader was John Smith. The Church of England was established as the ecclesiastical body. It was required that each male over sixteen years of age should pay annually ten pounds of tobacco and one bushel of corn for the support of the clergy. Very soon there arose trouble in the little body. John Smith had his enemies, and they were not slow to express their hostility. One of the members of this colony was Sandys, who wrote the first English work ever written in the Western Hemisphere—a "Translation of Ovid's Metamorphoses." By trouble with the Indians, by depletion through disease, and from other causes, the colonists were reduced to great need, and but for a timely reinforcement would probably have become extinct. The first stage of difficulty having passed, the period of earnest practical work began. John Smith wrote back to England a letter disabusing the public mind of its dream of gold from Virginia by saying, "Nothing is to be expected thence but by labor." Corn was planted, houses were built, tobacco-fields were cultivated, and in fifteen years the number of colonists, increased by later energetic arrivals, numbered five thousand people.

3. **The Plymouth Colony** arrived in 1620, at Cape Cod.

These men were the boldest, most original, and most devout of all the organized colonies which landed on the American shore. The Pilgrims were revolutionists in the highest moral sense. The little company of Brownists, who were Separatists from the Established Church, sailed from Scrooby, in Lincolnshire, England, for Holland, intending to make that country their permanent abode. They remained in Amsterdam one year, then went to Leyden, and lived twelve years, where they had a church of three hundred communicants, and finally determined to try their fortunes in the New World; or, as Canning has said, "They turned to the New World to redress the balance of the Old." Two of their number—Robert Cushman and John Carver—were sent to England to secure a patent to unite with the Virginia Colony. A patent seems to have been received, but it did them no good. The Pilgrims left Leyden for England, and set sail from Plymouth in the *Mayflower* and the *Speedwell*. The latter vessel proved unseaworthy, and returned. The *Mayflower* crossed the ocean, and on November 9, 1620, she dropped anchor at Cape Cod. John Robinson had been the pastor in Leyden. He remained in Europe, but comforted his flock by sympathetic administration until they sailed and by pastoral letters after their departure. The Plymouth colonists suffered from disease, the inroads of the Indians, and the scarcity of food. They "knew not at night where to have a bit in the morning." Eight months after their arrival they removed permanently from Cape Cod, and settled on the western side of Massachusetts Bay, where they built a town, and called it Plymouth, after the last place which they had left in England.

4. **The Colony of Massachusetts Bay** was secured by

THE ENGLISH COLONIZATION. 15

English Puritans in 1629. Probably Charles I. would never have granted this Puritan request but for its character—permission to leave his realm. Then, too, he may have been influenced by the fact that James I., in November, 1620, had granted a charter to forty persons for a belt of territory between the fortieth and forty-eighth degrees of north latitude, extending from the Atlantic to the Pacific. This charter had been dissolved, and the new charter for Massachusetts Bay might safely take its place. Winthrop, with a company of eight hundred men, was the Massachusetts leader. He said, "I shall call that my country where I may most glorify God and enjoy the presence of my dearest friends." The Massachusetts men consisted of the middle class of English Puritans. Some were lawyers and members of other learned professions. Others were good farmers, men of large landed estates, Oxford scholars, and divines. Among the clergy were such intellectual giants as Cotton, Hooker, and Roger Williams.

5. **Rapid Increase.**—A body of two hundred colonists was already established at Salem. Winthrop's men united with them. Some seven hundred more colonists followed in the wake of Winthrop's ships. There was no hope whatever for any favor in England. The whole trend of royal authority was against the Puritans. Archbishop Laud was persecuting all non-conformists, without even the pretence of mercy. The Puritans looked to America as probably their only safe asylum. There was not a Puritan fireside in England where the hope of going to America was not entertained. During the ten or eleven years preceding the Long Parliament not less than two hundred ships left England, bearing towards the Western World twenty thousand Puritans. "Farewell, dear England," they

said, as the English coast faded from their view, while Winthrop's followers wrote back to the less fortunate brethren: "Our hearts shall be fountains of tears for your everlasting welfare, when we shall be in our poor cottages in the wilderness."

6. **The Amalgamation of the Colonies** of Plymouth and Massachusetts Bay was only a question of time. The two bodies differed essentially. The Plymouth men had no royal authority; were without charter; cared nothing for it; rejoiced in their independence; were outside of the Church of England; indeed, carried a free lance from the hour they left Scrooby for Holland. The men of Massachusetts Bay were a political body. The charter was to the Governor and Company of Massachusetts Bay in New England. They had large authority, and could admit new members on any terms they pleased. They professed strong attachment to the king, but enjoyed the liberty of an ocean between Massachusetts Bay and Charles I.

7. **A Serious Question** now arose: How would these two colonies stand related to each other? While Massachusetts Bay Colony had royal credentials, and was of greater number, the Plymouth Colony was older; had been making laws; expanding; studying the Indian character; organizing a church; developing, under Miles Standish, a military system; in fact, founding a nation. The smaller body gave strength to the larger. Whatever bonds held the Massachusetts men to dear England were now seen to be useless. In due time the two bodies were marvellously alike—all were separatists from the Establishment; all met together in ecclesiastical synods; the civil and the religious life became a unit. Little Plymouth had proved stronger than large Massachusetts Bay.

Chapter V.

MARYLAND, PENNSYLVANIA, AND OTHER ENGLISH COLONIES.

1. **The Colony of Maryland** was the only English colony of the Roman Catholic faith. Sir Charles Calvert (Lord Baltimore) had been a Protestant, but became a Roman Catholic. England was, therefore, no place for him. He, with a company of the same communion, secured a charter for the founding of a colony in Maryland. In order to carry out his plan he had the shrewdness to see that a colony of Roman Catholics alone would not be tolerated. The first Lord Baltimore died before his charter received the royal seal, but the pledges were made good to his son Cecil, the second Lord Baltimore. Freedom was granted to all Christian faiths. The first Maryland law was: "No person within this province professing to believe in Jesus Christ shall be in any ways troubled, molested, or discountenanced for his or her religion, or in the free exercise thereof." This was the first declaration of perfect religious liberty in the New World. The colonists, about two hundred in number, arrived in 1634. The colony was called Maryland, after Henrietta Maria, the wife of Charles I. The first stage in its history was prosperous. While the Catholics were at the outset in the majority, the Protestants increased so rapidly that they soon gained the upper hand. By the end of the century the Protestants had control.

The Church of England became the faith of the colony. Laws were even enacted against the Roman Catholics.

2. Other Southern Colonies were now organized. North Carolina was settled mainly through the Virginia colonists, who went thither, introduced their own usages and laws, and established the Church of England as the faith of the colony. South Carolina also received colonial settlers from Virginia. It began to be a colonial field about 1670. Its laws were at first very liberal, all faiths being protected with equal favor. But in time the Church of England gained greatest strength, and became the established ecclesiastical system. Georgia was colonized by the humane Oglethorpe in 1732. He brought thither a colony consisting mostly of English debtors. At this time one of the most badly treated of all classes in England were the debtors. The mere inability to pay a debt was the ground of grossest inhumanity. These people were invited to join Oglethorpe, and they became the basis of the future population of Georgia. Persecuted Protestants from Austria settled later in Georgia. Jews were welcomed. In Oglethorpe's colony were John and Charles Wesley, who came as missionaries to the Indians.

3. The First Colonists in Pennsylvania were Swedes, Dutch, and English. But the first charter for a regular colony was granted to William Penn, by Charles II., in 1681. Though Penn was a Quaker, and his faith prevailed among the people whom he led to Pennsylvania, all communions were granted full liberty. Penn visited Germany, and large numbers of Germans accepted his invitation and settled in the new colony. Penn's just and humane attitude towards the Indians made them the friends of his colony. He bought of them the land where Philadelphia now stands. They promised: "We will live in love with William Penn and his children, and with his children's children as long as the moon and sun endure." The Quakers, who were persecuted everywhere else in America except Rhode Island, came to Pennsylvania. It was the refuge for all the persecuted along the Atlantic coast.

4. **The Scotch-Irish** became an important factor in the new Protestant colonization. It is probable that the Scotch stood next to the Irish in determining the religious quality of the great body of American colonists. Charles II., when he became king, forgot the service which the Scotch had done for his succession to the English throne, and immediately began to persecute them. They were Presbyterians, and in sympathy with the Puritans. That was enough for Charles II., who, being a Stuart, was not bound by a sense of honor or obligation. He abolished Presbyterianism in Scotland, and established the Court of High Commission. Persecution of the Presbyterians in Scotland and the north of Ireland became the order of the day. They saw that their only hope lay in hastening to America. They fled the country in large numbers during the reigns of both Charles II. and James II. They went to no particular colony, but only where they had an opportunity to exercise their rights of conscience. Some went to Maine, but the larger number went to East New Jersey and Pennsylvania. They went westward in Pennsylvania along the Susquehanna valley, entered the Cumberland valley, and continued into Virginia, North Carolina, and Kentucky.

5. **Other Colonists** arrived from various parts of Europe. The Moravians, under the guidance of Zinzen-

dorf, came to Pennsylvania, organized societies in Philadelphia, and made Bethlehem, in Pennsylvania, the centre of their work. Moravians also settled in Connecticut, North Carolina, and, to a limited extent, also in Georgia. The Salzburger Protestants, driven out of Austria because of their faith, were granted land and all civil and religious rights by Oglethorpe in Georgia, where they aided largely in the development of that colony. Protestant Poles joined in the colonial current to America. Italian Protestants came over, and settled in New York, where the people of the Reformed Church extended hospitality to them and took collections in the churches for their relief.

Chapter VI.

CONTINENTAL COLONIES: DUTCH, SWEDES, HUGUENOTS, AND OTHER PROTESTANTS.

1. **The Dutch** were among the most daring navigators of this period. Rejoicing in their new independence, they sailed over distant seas, and took possession of new territory with all the vigor and heroism which they had displayed in enduring the siege of Leyden, and resisting the oppression of Spain. Their present possessions in the East Indies are still a testimony to their success on the Oriental seas. "The Truth of the Christian Religion," by Grotius, written for the heathen world, was one of the strongest, as it was one of the first, pleas of the times for a universal gospel. America came in for its share of Dutch colonial enterprise. The discovery of the North River by Henry Hudson gave his country the first claim to Manhattan Island, now the site of New York. The Dutch erected there the first cluster of houses in 1614, which was meant as a trading-station with the Indians. They established other posts along the coast, but this was always the centre of their trade, which consisted chiefly in the exchange of European articles with the Indians for furs.

2. **Little Dutch communities** were established on Long Island, Staten Island, along the Hudson River, westward along the Mohawk, and in New Jersey along the Passaic valley. They organized their first church in

New York in 1619. A church in Albany was erected about the same time. The established religion was the Reformed. The ministers, such as Frelinghuysen and others, who were educated and talented men, came directly from Holland. The Dutch language was used in the pulpit, and even continued in some cases down to 1764. When New Netherlands was ceded to the English, the name of New York was given to the town and the colony. The population of the town, at the time of the cession, was about ten thousand.

3. **The Colony of New Sweden** was established by Swedes, who settled on the banks of the Delaware in 1638. They brought with them the Lutheran faith, and lost nothing of their Protestant attachment by removing to the New World. Gustavus Adolphus took special interest in the colony at its inception, but was killed on the victorious field of Lützen before its success was assured. The pastors of the colony paid special attention to the conversion of the Indians. Luther's Catechism was translated into the Indian tongue. Campanius and Acrelius sent back minute accounts of the progress of the colony, and their works are two of the best accounts of American colonization extant. There was early conflict with the Dutch, who asserted their claim to the Swedish territory. Peter Stuyvesant, Governor of New Netherlands, led an expedition against the Swedish Colony in 1655, which, after seventeen years of prosperous existence, now came to an end. But the Dutch ownership was brief. The same Stuyvesant, nine years later, hauled down the Dutch flag, surrendered to the English fleet, and New Amsterdam henceforth became New York.

4. **The French Huguenots** were an important part of the great body of incoming colonists. The Edict of

Nantes had been issued in the interest of the Protestants, who, in France, bore the name of Huguenots. It was not all they wished or merited, but it guaranteed certain civil and religious rights. When this Edict was revoked by Louis XIV., it was a signal for violent persecution. As many as half a million of French Protestants were driven out of the country. Some went to Holland, others to Germany, others to England, others to the Cape of Good Hope, and still others to America. As early as 1662, we find Jean Touton applying to the Massachusetts Bay Colony for permission to live there. He was granted the privilege. In 1686 a tract of eleven thousand acres of land in Massachusetts was ceded to a Huguenot colony, who settled at Oxford. In 1656 a body of Huguenots was welcomed at New Amsterdam. They founded the town of New Rochelle, on the East River. In 1666 there were Huguenots in Maryland, and in Virginia in 1671. In 1679 Charles II. of England sent two shiploads of Huguenots to South Carolina. In 1703 the Huguenots were naturalized as citizens in New York. The Huguenots who came to America, and thus distributed themselves in various parts of the colonies, had neither the ambition nor the taste for political colonization. Their sole purpose was freedom for life and faith. No purer Europeans have ever landed on the American coast than the Huguenots of France. Their descendants have adorned every path of life. In war and in peace their names have been in the front rank of Christians and citizens.

5. **The Germans in Pennsylvania.** The German immigration to America arose out of the persecution of Protestants in the Palatinate by the troops of Louis XIV. of France. The French soldiers persecuted them

without mercy. All were stripped of their possessions, and many were killed. Those who escaped had to flee the country. Some fled to Northern Germany, where the Elector of Brandenburg gave them a cordial welcome to Berlin. Others fled to Ireland. Some settled in England. But the general wish was to reach America. Some settled along the Hudson and the Mohawk. But the most of the Germans went to Pennsylvania, distributing themselves from Philadelphia into the interior of the state. The new colony, founded by William Penn, received large accessions from the Germans. While they did not become Quakers, they were equally welcomed, and became an important population of the new colony. Before the Revolution nearly all the Germans coming to America were Protestants. From Maine to Georgia they rapidly distributed themselves, uniting with the colonies in all their great interests, and helping to plant political liberty and an unfettered gospel.

Chapter VII.

THE PROVIDENTIAL PLANTING.

1. **When the American Planting began,** Europe was undergoing a complete transformation. The old conditions were breaking up, and a new departure was at hand. The English language had taken the place of the Norman French in England, and represented the popular drift towards larger political and religious liberty. In 1362, the English was ordered in the courts of English law. Wyclif's tracts were in the newly liberated tongue, and gave the people their first taste of truth in a language dear to their hearts. Chaucer was the first poet to present in English verse the coming larger life of the Anglo-Saxon intellect. English and Continental commerce was extended all over the face of the world. Caxton had made the printing-press the possession of the Anglo-Saxon race. The people of England now first saw the industrial field opening before them. Agriculture showed signs of becoming what it was in republican Rome—the best of all manual employments. The eastern coast of England was learning from the Flemish weavers, who were now their guests, those lessons of manufacturing which to this day have made England a large producer for all lands.

2. **Protestants** were conquering on the great fields of Germany, England, and Scandinavia. Even when they failed in liberty, their faith in final triumph failed not.

The Puritans, burning with shame at the royal deception, looked westward to find their true home. When the colonies in America were planted, both from England and the Continent, the people who constituted them arrived at the moment of European awakening. They brought the best aspirations of the Old World, and determined to realize them in the New. The hour of American colonization was the fittest one, in all modern times, for the New World to receive the best which the Old World had to give.

3. **The Territorial Distribution** of the colonists was not less providential. The territorial successes of the Spanish knights, and Jesuit fathers who accompanied them, were confined to a doubtful settlement in Florida, to the great province of New Spain (Mexico), and to a strip of the Pacific coast. The French Roman Catholic explorers and their Jesuit fathers were limited to Indian evangelization and an uncertain territory along the St. Lawrence, the northern chain of Lakes, and the Mississippi valley. The great English field of colonization lay between these two. It is the temperate belt of North America—the region which nature had fitted for the most aggressive mission in Western civilization. Spain's field has become more contracted as the centuries have passed. She now holds no foot of land on the North American continent. Louisiana passed from her hands into French possession, and in 1803 the French sold it to the United States. This purchase, made to fill the empty exchequer of Napoleon I., placed the Mississippi in the possession of the United States, and made the whole domain from that river to the Pacific a future certainty. The French bade fair to own all Canada. The ownership was at last reduced to the fortunes of one battle—that of Quebec,

THE PROVIDENTIAL PLANTING. 27

in 1759. Here the English conquered. This culmination of a long and bitter series of wars between France and England made the English the possessors of that immense tract lying between the United States and the polar seas, and extending from the Atlantic to the Pacific. The war with Mexico, closing in 1848, gave the United States the great state of Texas, which covers an area of two hundred and seventy-five thousand square miles. The territory now protected by the flag of the United States is a rich inheritance. Every part of it is a witness to the providential guidance of our fathers to these shores, and a reminder of the obligation upon their posterity to mould our immigrant population into a righteous citizenship.

Chapter VIII.

POLITICAL FRAMEWORK OF THE COLONIES.

1. No Uniformity in Authority is perceptible in the first colonial organizations. Each arose out of the exigencies of the time. The caprice of the ruler, the necessity of the emigration because of suffering at home, and the favor of the leaders with the court and the people, were each a factor which determined the nature of the new government. The colonies, when once established in the New World, were simply a group of local governments, a cluster of diverse republics, each dependent more or less on the order of the government at home. But in all there was larger liberty than either the colonists or their rulers had anticipated. The Atlantic added new and deeper colors to the aspirations for freedom.

2. There were Four Varieties of Colonial Authority and government. One was the Charter governments. This was the type of Massachusetts Bay, Rhode Island, and Connecticut. Plymouth, without the formality of charter, possessed the same authority. Large liberty was allowed, and larger liberty was taken than was granted. While there was a general accounting to the home government, these colonies had the power of assessing their own taxes, regulating their ecclesiastical system, and determining their colonial legislature. The governor had to account to England for his conduct. But the Assembly chose his Council, and the Assembly was elected by popular suffrage. This large liberty to the popular will was the one fatal cause of dissolving the subjection of the provinces to England. It bred the Revolution, and the Republic.

3. **The Provincial and Royal Grants** were the second form of authority. Here was the closest relation to the British Crown. Both the governor and the council were appointed by the king. There were two houses of legislature, the council being the upper one. The lower house were elected by the people. New Hampshire, New Jersey, Virginia, the two Carolinas, and Georgia were under this form. The third were the Proprietary Grants. This was a grant to the proprietors, who could appoint their own governor and convene the legislative body. But there was provision that no act should be done which would interfere with the original authority of the crown. Pennsylvania, Maryland, and Delaware were under this form. In appearance, this was the most liberal of all the forms of colonial government. But New England was so managed by the people and their governors that they *took* the most authority. The fourth class consisted of irregular colonies, which had no royal authority whatever, but settled among others who did possess it. The Huguenots, the first Germans, the Salzburg Emigrants, the Moravians, and the few Polish and Waldensian Protestants belonged to this class. They identified themselves with the interests of the colonists who received them and gave them hospitality.

4. **Religious Liberty** under these various forms was very diverse. Pennsylvania and Delaware had it in the fullest sense. The Church of England was established in Virginia, Maryland, New Hampshire, New Jersey, the Carolinas, and Georgia. But even here

there were varieties of liberty. In Virginia there was only little, but in Georgia both Jew and Gentile had equal protection from the law. While in New York the Reformed Church was established by the West India Company as early as 1640, there was practical freedom of conscience. When the English became possessors of New Amsterdam, they were tolerant to all faiths. Of all the New England colonies, Rhode Island was the first to declare perfect religious toleration. This was due entirely to the leadership of Roger Williams. He was at first a Puritan, but, adopting Baptist and Independent views, he was dismembered, and, but for timely escape, would have been forcibly exported back to England.

Chapter IX.

CHURCH GOVERNMENT IN THE COLONIES.

1. The Church Laws in New England proceeded directly from the civil authority. The support of the clergy, the establishment of churches, and the duties of the governing body were prescriptions of colonial legislation. In the first Court of Assistants for Massachusetts Bay, on August 23, 1630, the first question was the support of the clergy. In the same year the first church in Boston and Charlestown was organized, and Wilson was ordained to the ministry. There was, considering the population, a rapid increase of churches. In fifteen years after the landing at Plymouth the tenth church was organized.

2. The Church of England being the established faith for the most of the colonies, there was no separate colonial legislation for ecclesiastical order. All that the governors and councils and legislative bodies needed to do was to provide for the support of the clergy and the erection of edifices. There was universal scarcity of ministers. One of the great causes of the religious decline in Virginia was the want of clerical supplies. All who were in office had to come over as ordained men.

3. The New England Synods were the source of ecclesiastical doctrine until a definite order of local church government was adopted. Cotton's book, "The Keys," was the guide. The first New England Synod met in

1637. But this was a tentative measure. No platform of discipline or doctrine was established by it. In 1646 a request was made to the legislature of Massachusetts that it could call a synod for the purpose of establishing a "Platform of Church Discipline." Objections were made, many people fearing tyrannical measures. In 1647 the synod met, by order of the legislature, and Cotton, Partridge, and Richard Mather were appointed to frame a platform.

4. **The Cambridge Platform.** In 1648 the celebrated Cambridge Platform was adopted as the report of the committee. The Westminster Confession of Faith was adopted as the doctrinal basis of the synod, and "commended to the churches of Christ among us, and to the honored court, as worthy of their due consideration and acceptance." It declared that the members of the visible Church are saints; that their children are holy; that the offices of pastor and of teacher are distinct; that the special work of pastor is to attend to exhortation and of the teacher to doctrine; that the office of ruling elder is distinct from those of pastor and teacher; that church officers are to be chosen by the Church, and ordained by imposition of hands; that the requisite for membership is repentance of sin and faith in Jesus Christ; and that synods and councils must determine controversies of faith and cases of conscience, and bear witness against mal-administration and corruption in doctrines and manners. In 1679 another synod confirmed this Platform. As all these synods met by order of the legislature, and were approved by the same body, the Platform itself had all the force of civil law, and was the order in courts of law.

5. **The Reforming Synod**—the one of 1679—was held for the special purpose of taking action in regard to

the sufferings of the New England colonists. Probably at no time in the colonial or national history has there been such an accumulation of disasters as at this time. The Indian depredations were widespread and devastating; storms along the coast had wrecked many vessels; droughts had cut off the harvests; pestilence had raged in various localities; and fire had spread havoc in the homes and among industries. The legislature called on the churches to send elders and messengers to meet in synod, and discuss two questions—What are the prevailing evils of New England? and, What is to be done that these evils may be removed? The synod concluded that the disastrous phenomena were due to the wickedness of the people, such as decay of godliness; spirit of contention; young people not mindful of the obligations of baptism; profanation of the sabbath; profaning of God's name; neglect of prayer and scriptural reading; intemperance; and forsaking the churches. The synod also declared that the members of the churches must advance in piety, renew their vows, support the schools, and cry fervently for the "rain of righteousness." The result was, that "this synod was followed with many of the good effects which were desired and expected by its friends."

6. **The Final Confession of Faith.** The Boston Synod of 1680, of which Increase Mather was moderator, adopted a Confession of Faith. With few exceptions, it was the same as that adopted by the Westminster Assembly, and later by the General Assembly of Scotland. It was, in fact, only more elaborate, the same Confession as the Cambridge Platform, adopted in 1648. A reason was urged for adopting the European Reformed Confessions, "that so they might not only with one heart, but with one mouth, glorify God and our

Lord Jesus Christ." Henceforth this was the doctrinal basis of the churches of colonial New England.

7. The Saybrook Platform was adopted by the ministers and delegates of the Colony of Connecticut in 1708. The motion for a synod arose from a request of the trustees of Yale College in 1703. The Saybrook Platform was a repudiation of the Savoy and Westminster Confessions of Faith, and embodied a system of ecclesiastical government and discipline. It was passed by the legislative body as a law of the colony of Connecticut, and became the civil constitution for all the churches of the colony.

Chapter X.

EDUCATION.

1. The Educational Spirit of the first colonists was intense. The Virginia colony numbered among its members men who had been thoroughly educated, and whose associations and tastes fitted them for an appreciation of the value of education to their posterity. The New England colonists, while not from an equally elevated social position in the Old World, were far more devoted to literary pursuits, and were more keenly alive to the importance of culture for the well-being of the population. It was the authorship of the Pilgrims which caused their exile in Holland. They had written, and therefore they had to suffer. John Robinson, their pastor, was a disputant against Episcopius in the University of Leyden. His writings, which have been preserved, were such as to aid largely in moulding the New England mind in its most plastic period. Brewster was both publisher and author. The records of Winthrop, Morton, and others show the skill with which the first Puritans of New England knew how to use the pen.

2. Elementary Education. One of the first thoughts of the New England colonists was elementary education for their children. The first common school was established in New England about 1645, and became the herald of all the common schools in the United States. Instruction was gratuitous, the expenses being met by direct tax on the inhabitants of the town. Schools of various grades sprang up in all parts of the New England colonies, though Boston very early became the centre. In 1635 an appropriation was made for Pormont as schoolmaster. Six years afterwards the foundation was laid in the same place for the celebrated public Latin School. Academies sprang rapidly into existence. Here young men were prepared for Harvard, Yale, and similar institutions.

3. **The First Important Educational Movement in Virginia** was an undertaking to found the " University of Henrico," for the education of English and Indians. This began within a few years after the settlement in Jamestown. Friends in England took pains to collect funds for the purpose. The Bishop of London gave one thousand pounds sterling for the new institution of learning, and another contributor presented five hundred pounds for educating young Indians. The preacher at Henrico, the Rev. Mr. Bargrave, donated his library. A school preparatory to the University was proposed, to be located at St. Charles City, to be called the East India School, the first gift having been made by the officers and crew of an East India ship. This whole movement failed because of the Indian massacre of 1622. The colonists, however, never lost sight of the founding of a higher institution of learning. Occasionally they had to contend with the opposition of those who governed them. Sir William Berkeley, in 1670, resisted an application of the Lords of Plantation in the following language: "I thank God there are no schools nor printing, and I hope we shall not have them these one hundred years; for learning has brought disobedience and heresy and sects into the world, and printing has divulged them and

libels against the best government. God keep us from both!"

4. **Harvard College** was the first institution of advanced learning in the American colonies. It was founded in 1639, for the special purpose of a theological school, for the benefit of posterity, "fearing an illiterate ministry." The General Court had already voted four hundred pounds for a public school. The Rev. John Harvard, of Charlestown, made a bequest of over eighteen hundred dollars as an endowment to the school. He also donated three hundred and twenty volumes as the beginning of a library. It was called a college, and the name of Harvard, its principal benefactor, was given to it. The name of Newtown, where it was located, was changed to Cambridge, in honor of the University of Cambridge, where many of the New England Puritan fathers had been educated. The legislature ordered that the income of Charlestown ferry should be granted the college as a perpetual revenue. The Rev. Henry Dunster was appointed the president. The mottoes of the college were: *In Gloriam Christi* ("For the Glory of Christ"); *Christo et Ecclesiae* ("To Christ and his Church"). The college received its first charter in 1650. That the first idea of the founding of Harvard—as a theological school—was never lost sight of during its early period may be seen in the fact that during the first century of its history three hundred and seventeen of its alumni became ministers of the Gospel. This institution, and its great success, led to similar ones in other parts of New England. Yale followed in 1701; Brown, in 1764; Dartmouth, in 1769; Burlington, in 1791; and Bowdoin in 1795.

5. **William and Mary College** was the first successful attempt to establish an institution of high grade in

Virginia. It was founded in 1693. As Harvard College grew out of the great success of the pastoral labors of the Rev. Thomas Shepard, so the college of William and Mary grew out of the long and arduous labors of the Rev. Dr. Blair. This institution became the most important educational centre in all the Southern colonies. During the entire colonial period it was the place where many of the statesmen and clergy of Virginia were educated. Its power was felt, not only in that one colony, but in the leadership which led to the War of Independence.

6. **The Remaining Colonies** were far behind New England in educational measures. New York had its Dutch teachers early, but it was not until 1746 that its first great college—Columbia—was founded. Princeton, for New Jersey, was founded in the same year. Dickinson, at Carlisle, was established to meet the wants of the rural population in the valleys of the Cumberland and the Susquehanna. The first provision in Maryland for a school was in 1723. No school of college grade was established in Georgia or the Carolinas before the Revolution. Much of the instruction given throughout the Southern colonies was private. The planters took care to have good tutors from England brought over and placed in charge of their sons. The tutors lived on the plantations, in the families where they taught. Governesses were provided for the daughters of the planters. This method of education seems to have been preferred to the schools of higher grade. We cannot infer from the absence of such foundations in the South that education was neglected. For the great mass of the people there was no good provision. But for the more wealthy there was ample provision in this private system of instruction. The

planters had not only their tutors, but they were attentive to the introduction of the best works in all departments of European literature. The libraries in the homes of the planters of Virginia and other Southern colonies, during the colonial period, were in some cases magnificent. Books from the European press were constantly arriving. Besides, many young men went over to Europe for an education. The fashion of young Americans attending the foreign universities seems to have had its origin in the South, and particularly in South Carolina, during the colonial period.

Chapter XI.

INTOLERANCE IN THE COLONIES.

1. **The Intolerance of the Old World** was transferred, with modifications, to the New. The two colonies of Virginia and Plymouth represented the two great rival ecclesiastical bodies of England—the Established Church and the Non-Conformists. The Virginia colonists were of the Established Church. They had with them a clergyman, Hunt, of that body, and were under his pastoral care. The parish system was adopted, after the established model at home. The hostility in England to the Non-Conformists, of whom the Puritans were the largest portion, was reproduced in Virginia, and exercised without any show of serious opposition. The New England colonists had suffered keenly from the intolerance of Laud and the Crown at home. The Act of Uniformity of 1662 had thrown out of their livings two thousand English Non-Conformist preachers, for the sole reason that they would not submit to re-ordination and full endorsement of the Book of Common Prayer. The Puritan exile to America was the child of bitter persecution. The colonists had grown into solidarity and strength under the lash. It is not surprising that when these Puritan colonists now enjoyed liberty they should not forget the oppressor's hand, nor have a very kindly feeling towards those who had persecuted them. Their intolerance was their means for guarding against a new mastery in the New World.

2. The New England Intolerance was directed against all who differed in religious matters from the colonists. The Massachusetts and New Haven colonies were particularly severe against the Quakers. In 1658 the General Court of New Haven passed a severe law against the Quakers, as a body "who take upon them that they are immediately sent from God, are infallibly assisted by the Spirit, who speak and write blasphemous opinions, despise government, and the order of God in Church and Commonwealth." The penalty of bringing in any known Quakers, or "other blasphemous heretics," was a fine of fifty pounds. If a Quaker should come for a business purpose, he should appear before a magistrate and receive license to transact his business, and in case of first disobedience should be whipped, imprisoned, put to labor, and deprived of converse with any one; for a second offence, should be branded on one hand with the letter H, imprisoned, and put to labor; for a third offence his other hand should be branded, and he be put to labor and imprisoned; and for a fourth offence he should be imprisoned, kept to labor until sent away at his own charge, and his tongue bored through with a red-hot iron. This law continued in existence but two years. Stiles says, that notwithstanding this law no witch or Quaker was ever punished in the New Haven colony. The Massachusetts laws were very severe against the Quakers. The records show that thirty were imprisoned, fined, or whipped; twenty-two were banished; three had an ear cut off; and four were hung. The same colony was intolerant of the Baptists. The first members of that communion were fined and imprisoned. The Maine laws were not less intolerant. The first Episcopalians in Connecticut were cast into prison.

3. **Rhode Island**, though established as a colony granting full religious liberty, soon forgot its first principle. Its charter ran: "None are at any time to be molested for any difference in matters of religion." But its first Assembly, in 1663, declared against the admission of Roman Catholics as freemen, or to be chosen as colonial officers.

4. **The Expulsion of Roger Williams** from Salem was a notable case of colonial intolerance. He gave great provocation, however, and the wonder is that he did not fare worse than suffer banishment. He was a Puritan preacher, and arrived with the Salem Colony in 1631. He demanded that the Church in Boston should repent publicly of the sin of remaining in communion with the Church of England before coming to America. This the Church in Boston refused to do, and Williams refused to join the Church. The magistrates refused to settle him as pastor. He therefore moved to Plymouth, where he became an assistant pastor. He returned to Salem and succeeded Skelton as pastor, but his permanent settlement was opposed by the magistrates on the ground that he had taught that "it is not unlawful for an unregenerate man to pray; that the magistrate has nothing to do in matters of the first table; that there should be a general and unlimited toleration of all religions; that to punish a man for following the dictates of his conscience was persecution; that the patent granted by Charles was invalid, and an instrument of injustice which they ought to renounce, being injurious to the natives, the king of England having no power to dispose of their lands to his own subjects." As a result, Williams was banished. He fled to Rhode Island, where he founded the present city of Providence, which he so called

"from a sense of God's merciful providence to him in his distress."

5. The Real Ground of Williams's Banishment.—The case of Roger Williams has produced a large literature and a wide difference of opinion. His manner was unfortunate. A man of gentler method might have escaped punishment. But it is likely that his attack on the title of the colony was the vital point of his offending. The New England colonists would allow no word against their just claim to their colony. They had suffered too much already to be running any risk as to the ownership of their dearly-bought acres.

6. The Virginia Colony compelled all persons to attend the parish worship. Roman Catholics, Quakers, and all Dissenters were prohibited from settling in the colony, and people of every country who had not been Christians at home were condemned to slavery. There seems to have been more leniency at first than later. In 1642, owing to the few clergymen, a petition went from Virginia to the Plymouth Colony to send down some Puritan preachers. Knolls and James were sent in answer to the request. But they were not permitted to remain long. Fears of a large influx, and especially of new opinions, seem to have been entertained; for these men were sent back, and their followers were scattered. In 1661 there was a rigid enforcement of the laws against Quakers and all others who were not of the Established Church. When the dissenting bodies increased, the same prohibition was observed. Moravians, Baptists, Presbyterians, "New Lights," and others were persecuted. In 1747 the Rev. Mr. Davis was sent to labor in Virginia. He was a wise, learned, and skilful man. He was very successful. His character and conduct were such as to commend him to all the people. He placed the Presbyterian Church in Virginia on a secure footing.

7. **Maryland and New York.**—The original Roman Catholic colony of Maryland underwent important changes from the beginning. The liberty of all to settle there was made use of to such extent that, by 1704, the non-Catholics were in the majority. An act was passed by the General Assembly to prevent an increase of Roman Catholics. This remained in force until 1776, when full religious liberty was restored. The Reformed Church was the established faith in the early history of New York. Quakers were fined and imprisoned. In 1656 the governor, Stuyvesant, forbade any other meetings than the Reformed. Baptists were persecuted. When the English came into possession of New Amsterdam (New York), they were tolerant of the Reformed Church, and in one case the same building was used for the Reformed and the Episcopal services. But this toleration was limited at first to the Reformed. Members of other communions received little favor. The first Presbyterian preachers, for example, Mackenzie and Hampton, were fined and imprisoned for preaching in a private house.

8. **The Grounds of Opposition** to the Roman Catholics are not hard to find. They are the only body which was everywhere opposed, except for a time in Maryland, and all the while in Pennsylvania. The extensive missions in Canada, with the line of missions in the West extending down to the Gulf, indicated a progress among the Indians which no Protestant body had met with. The relations of the Roman Catholics with the Indians were of the most cordial kind. The Indians were taught by them to believe that the

English were their enemies. The Puritans had good ground for hostility to the Roman Catholics in England; and, when to this was added the Indian opposition to the New England colonists by the Roman Catholic missions, it can occasion no surprise that everywhere the Roman Catholic was regarded as not only an ecclesiastical opponent, but a civil enemy. Down to the Revolution there was almost a universal opposition to Roman Catholics on the part of the colonists—in New England very decided, but in the Southern colonies less. Only after the Revolution were all confessions in full liberty of civil and religious rights. The great Roman Catholic immigration then set in, and soon the people of the Romish communion began, by labor and by numbers, to make ample amends for the early proscription.

Chapter XII.

Religious Life of the Colonies.

1. The Zeal of the First Colonists was intense and steady. No material embarrassment was permitted to obscure the original idea of colonization—namely, an open field for spiritual life. Extensive revivals prevailed throughout New England. The later colonists were received by the earlier groups with a cordial spiritual salutation. The first generation of Protestant American citizens took better care of new immigrants, and more rapidly incorporated them into the religious life of the country, than any succeeding generation has done. Schools were founded, churches were built, and large plans made for the conversion of the Indians. The prevailing idea of the Puritan colonies was, that they had the mission of building up great religious commonwealths, and solving in the New World the religious problems which could not be solved in the Old. This period of religious fervor continued to 1660, when a season of decline began, which continued down to 1720. The decline was induced by the devastating Indian wars, the witchcraft delusion, and the political agitations arising out of the oppressive measures of the British government.

2. The New England Preachers were able guides. Many of them had come from the English universities, and brought with them great literary skill, an intimate acquaintance with theological controversy, and a practical knowledge of the dangers of political oppression to religious life. Wilson, Cotton, Shepard, the Mathers, Philips, Higginson, and Skelton wielded the colony of Massachusetts Bay at will. The religious spirit absorbed all others. The preacher was the real governor. No public measure had any chance of success without the clerical support. Brewster in Plymouth, Hooker in Connecticut, Davenport in New Haven, Roger Williams in Rhode Island, and Hunt and Whitaker in Virginia, were the giants of their time. Political preaching was the order of the day. The Old Testament was searched for parallels of duty whenever a war against the Indians was to be fought, or a new British aggression was to be resisted, or pestilence, famine, witchcraft, or earthquakes were to be wisely interpreted, and guarded against in the future. Books on the current questions were multiplied. The printing-press of New England was the powerful battery ever thundering against evils existing or apprehended.

3. **The Great Awakening** began about 1735. Its first indications were seen in the wonderful effects of the preaching of Jonathan Edwards in Northampton, Mass. Whitefield came over from England, and made several tours through the Atlantic colonies. His preaching attracted multitudes, and the numerous converts through his preaching united with the non-episcopal churches. The number converted through his American ministration has been estimated as high as fifty thousand. Prince, Frelinghuysen, Finley, and the brothers Tennent of New Jersey, and Davis and Blair of Virginia, and others, contributed greatly to the spiritual result. All the churches had their earnest leaders. The effects of the great revival, which

extended from New Hampshire down to the Carolinas, were immediately seen. A new spirit of toleration thrilled every nerve of the colonial churches. New church edifices were erected. Many young men entered the ministry. Schools of all grades sprang into existence, and large funds were brought from their hiding-places and cast into the Lord's treasury. Religious books multiplied. Even the conservative Benjamin Franklin rejoiced to publish the sermons of Whitefield and Tennent, the Westminster Catechism, and the powerful tracts of John Wesley.

4. **The Writings of Puritans** in the Old World were promptly introduced into the New. Special pains were taken by the New England fathers to get early copies of the great works which their co-religionists in England were producing. The works of Baxter were reproduced in Boston, and brought promptly into the early New England homes. The songs of Watts were reprinted in many editions, and were sung in the most distant settlements. Bunyan was beloved, and became a household companion. For Milton's poetry there was little taste; but his political tracts were great favorites, for they were thunderbolts against tyranny. Of all the writers who contributed most to found the republic of the United States, Milton probably bears away the palm.

5. **The Southern Colonies,** though visited by Whitefield, did not share extensively in the great revival of the middle of the eighteenth century. The Protestant Episcopal Church in Virginia did not give a cordial welcome to the revival influences. The preaching in Virginia pulpits was generally formal, and on topics merely moral. Morgan Morgan and Devereux Jarratt were notable exceptions.

Chapter XIII.

COLONIAL WORSHIP AND USAGES.

1. **The Sermon was the Chief Part** in the Puritan service. The preacher was supplied with an hourglass, and it was not uncommon for it to be reversed twice during his discourse, when a new start was made each time. There was a wide range to the sermon. The Old Testament was a favorite part of the Scriptures for subjects. The formal divisions, extending to great numerical length, were the rule. The people were kept awake, if not by the sermon, at least by the tithing-man, who walked around at fit times with his pole, and touched the offenders on the head. The colonial period was the golden age of political preaching in New England. Soldiers about to start against the Indians were addressed in the church. All unusual phenomena of nature were recognized in the discourses. A comet was not too small an affair to produce several sermons by Cotton Mather, which in due time were clothed with the dignity of print. The Election Sermon was a permanent institution. The Monday Lecture in Boston was only a continuation of the Sabbath.

2. **The Prayer** was long. The congregation stood during prayer. There was first an invocation. But the long prayer was second in importance only to the sermon. It was as formal as the sermon, the dif-

ference being that the divisions of the prayer were not announced. The subjects of the prayer were of great number. Few, indeed, we may well imagine, were the public events which were not considered in the course of the "long prayer." In some cases the pastor made a halt in his prayer, which it was understood was intended to be improved by the more weary to sit down. Dorchester says he has seen a manuscript volume of sermons of Rev. Thomas Clap (1725) which contains a "Scheme of Prayer," with five general divisions and two hundred and forty sub-heads. Sewall, in his "Diary," speaks of a fast-day service where, after three persons had prayed, and one had preached, "another prayed an hour and a half."

3. **The Singing** was congregational, and the psalm was lined by the ruling elder. The "Bay Psalm Book," printed in 1640, in Boston, was the universal favorite. The first two editions of this work were the Psalms of David as we find them in the Old Testament. But all subsequent editions were metrical. The "Psalterium Americanum" came into vogue, and was a great favorite in New England. It contained the musical notes. Great care was taken that the singing should be exceedingly simple, lest an approach might be made to the choral enormities of the Church of England, which to the Puritans was only a younger Church of Rome.

4. **Special Services** were held on Thanksgiving and fast days. The law required that all should attend these services, as well as those on the Sabbath, or pay a fine of five shillings for every absence. The services on Thanksgiving and fast days were the great occasions of the year. There was a general gathering up of themes which had excited public attention. The

preacher had before him the great officials of his town. In the churches of the larger towns, the same prominence was given to the service. The Governor and his Council were expected to be present. The preacher considered himself unfettered, and he made full use of his liberty.

5. **The Church Buildings** in the Southern colonies were modelled after the Church of England edifices in England. While small, there were the tower, the bell, the choir, and all the arrangements found in the smaller churches of England. But in New England there was a shunning of all ornamentation. Every reminder of the Church of England soon became an object to be avoided. The log church, which often served as fort for the gospel and for earthly weapons, was one of the first buildings thought of in the new town. No carpet or stove was present in the sanctuary, to remind of the repulsive luxuries of the wealthy across the sea, or to distract from the simple severity of the gospel. Even the Scripture lesson was avoided in New England during the seventeenth century, lest there might slip in a ritualistic tendency. The seats were guiltless of cushions. The female portion of the congregation sat on one side of the church, while the males occupied the other. The people from the country brought their lunch, and remained until the afternoon service was over.

Chapter XIV.

Missions to the Indians.

1. **The Conversion of the Indians** was one of the early objects of the colonists in America. The Virginia colony took the first steps. In 1619 a law was adopted requiring the instruction of Indian children. King Charles I. interested himself in their behalf, and directed that collections be taken in all the churches of England for training up and "educating infidel (Indian) children in the knowledge of God." But the most systematic and successful efforts in the direction of Indian evangelization were made in New England. In reply to a report from Plymouth to John Robinson, at Leyden, he wrote: "Oh, that you had converted some before you killed any!" In 1636 the Plymouth colony adopted an act for preaching the gospel to the Indians of the region. A special building was erected in connection with Harvard College for the education of Indian youth, while young men, the sons of colonists, were educated in Harvard for the special work of Indian evangelization. The chief tribes of Indians were the Mohegans, the Narragansetts, Pankunnawkuts, Massachusetts, Pawtuckets, Algonquins, and the Housatonics. The most successful of all the Indian schools in the colonies was founded in 1743, at Lebanon, Conn., by the Rev. Eleazer Wheelock. He received an Indian, Samson Occum, into his own house, and taught him five years. This Indian became a dis-

tinguished preacher, and went with the Rev. N. Whitaker to England, to collect funds for Wheelock's work, which had now developed into a school, where about twenty Indian youths were taught. It was called "Moor's Indian Charity School," from the man who gave a house and two acres of land to Wheelock for the school. Occum and Whitaker collected in England seven thousand pounds for the school. In 1770 Wheelock removed his school to Hanover, N. H., out of which has grown Dartmouth College.

2. **John Eliot, the Apostle to the Indians,** stands first of all men in devotion to the conversion and education of the Indians. He was born in England, educated in Cambridge University, and came to Boston in 1631. He was settled in Roxbury as pastor in 1632. He very early became interested in the Indians, and urged upon the General Assembly of Massachusetts the necessity of instructing them. The grandeur of Eliot's work lay in his own example. He hired a Pequot captive to instruct him in the Indian language, and in two years was able to preach in it. Owing to his representations, a society was established in England, called "A Corporation for the Promoting and Propagating the Gospel of Jesus Christ in New England." The sum of twelve thousand pounds was raised in England for Indian evangelization.

3. **Eliot's Evangelistic Labors** continued to the end of his life. He was about forty-two years of age before he began the study of the Indian (Mohegan) language, but used every possible means to perfect himself in it. With his usual modesty, he lamented to the end of his life his deficiency in mastering it. His first group of Indians was at Nonantum, now a part of Newton, near Boston. He then began to work at Ne-

ponsit, a part of the present Dorchester. He preached a number of years in both places, without compensation, and prayed in the Indian families. At no time in Eliot's life did his salary exceed fifty pounds. His eldest son preached several years to the Indians at Natick, Pakemit, the present Stoughton, and other places. The first Indian church was at Natick, where, in 1670, there were about fifty communicants. An Indian laborer, William Shawton, preached at Pakemit, and Tackuppa-willin preached at Hassanamenit, the present Grafton. Many societies of Indian worshippers sprang up in consequence of the labors of the two Eliots. In fourteen towns, within seventy miles of Boston, there were Indian services, where about eleven hundred Indians were under direct pastoral care. By the year 1664 it is estimated that there were in eastern Massachusetts about three thousand and six hundred "praying Indians." The Indians became not only moral, but many of them were devout Christians.

4. **The Literary Labors of John Eliot** are among the marvels of the colonial period. He learned from every quarter, and aimed to get at the finest shades of meaning in the Mohegan tongue. He translated Baxter's "Call" and Bayley's "Practice of Piety." He wrote grammars and primers and other small works, six in all, which, in literature, bear the name of "Eliot's Tracts." These works are now very rare. Copies of them, and, we believe, of all Eliot's works, are to be found in the Lenox Library, New York. The great literary achievement of Eliot was his Indian Bible. The New Testament was published in Boston, in 1661, and the Old Testament in 1663. A second edition appeared in 1680-85. This work was printed on type sent over from England by the Corporation for

the Promoting and Propagating the Gospel of Jesus Christ in New England. This was the first Bible printed in the New World, and is a monument to the philological skill and sublime devotion of John Eliot which will long continue to excite the admiration of men.

5. **Other Laborers in New England** were attentive to the spiritual needs of the Indians. In Plymouth Colony the Rev. Mr. Bourne had an Indian congregation of about five hundred on Cape Cod and the vicinity, and the Rev. John Cotton had a small congregation on Buzzard's Bay. The two Mayhews, father and son, made Martha's Vineyard the field of their labors, where they began their work about 1649. On the island of Nantucket there were, at the end of the seventeenth century, three churches and five congregations of "praying Indians." The Stockbridge Mission, in Massachusetts, was under the care of the Rev. Mr. Sargeant, one of the most devoted of all the New England laborers for the aboriginal tribes. He made lengthy journeys to other Indian tribes. He introduced manual trades and agriculture for the boys, and taught the girls the various duties of domestic life. His plan was largely that which our government has been too slow to learn—that, to build up the Indian character, the Indians must be taught the exercises and employments of the usual American citizen.

6. **Indian Evangelization in Other Colonies** was not neglected. The Reformed Church of Albany organized work among the Mohawks living along the Mohawk River about the time when Eliot began in New England. Schenectady became an important centre of missionary work, and the Liturgy of the Reformed Church was published in New York for the Mohawk tribe. The Protestant Episcopal Church of New York

published the Book of Common Prayer in the Mohawk tongue in 1715. Moore, Barclay, Andrews, Miles, and the Moravian Rauch were zealous missionaries among the Indians along the Hudson and the Mohawk. David Brainerd, in 1742, began work among the Indians at Kinderhook, near the Hudson, but his chief labor was on the Susquehanna. His career covered the brief period of about four years; but such was his devotion and courage that, though he was but thirty years old at the time of his death, his name will ever be associated with Eliot as a master-workman in the difficult field of Indian evangelization. What Henry Martyn was to India, David Brainerd has been to the American Indians. Hawley, Forbes, Kirkland, and Spencer were strong and successful laborers among the Six Nations. Hunt, Whitaker, and Thorpe distinguished themselves in Virginia for labors in behalf of the education and conversion of the Indians. But this work came to an end through a massacre of the whites by the Indians. John and Charles Wesley worked for a while as Indian missionaries in Georgia.

Chapter XV.

THEOLOGICAL MOVEMENTS.

1. The Puritan Mind was intensely theological. The experiences of the Pilgrims in the Old World had been such as to make them thinkers on fundamental doctrinal themes. The Brownists owed their existence as a separatist community to their divergence from the prevailing doctrines of the Established Church. The great Arminian controversy in Holland was in progress in Leyden during their residence there. John Robinson, their spiritual guide, was a warm disputant on the Calvinistic side. Their theological tendency was not thrown into the background by their immigration to America. The early Puritan preachers were skilful theologians. The sermon was often a mere section out of dogmatic theology. The future theological integrity of the colonies seems to have been prominent in the minds of all the spiritual leaders, and not to have been forgotten by the civil administrators. The frequent synods busied themselves fully as much with theological adjustments as with measures for parish government.

2. The Hutchinsonian Controversy arose out of the extreme views of a capable woman, Ann Hutchinson. While she was the leader, she was largely assisted by her brother-in-law, Wheelwright. She was described as a "gentlewoman of nimble wit and voluble tongue, of eminent knowledge in the Scriptures, great charity, and notable helpfulness in cases of need among her own sex." She claimed great attainments in spiritual life, and was very impressive in declaring her extreme views. She held that justification is produced by direct revelation or impression; that there is at once a perfect union between the Holy Ghost and the justified individual; that the Holy Ghost dwells in the justified one in person; that henceforth such an individual is as incapable of sinning as the Holy Ghost himself; that the letter of the Scriptures is subordinate, being only a covenant of works; and that the Spirit must be looked to for the covenant of grace. Her followers carried her views to still greater extravagance: that Christ himself is a part of the new creature; that Christ and the new creature are personally one; that a man is justified before he believes; that believers are not compelled to obey the divine law; that the Sabbath is the same as other days; that the soul is not immortal until it becomes united to Christ; that the final doom of the wicked is annihilation; that there is no resurrection of the body; and that the ground of all salvation is assurance by immediate revelation.

3. The Rapid Spread of the Hutchinsonian views was due largely to the great ability of Mrs. Hutchinson herself, and her influence with leading men in the Boston Church, of which she was a member. Many of the leading people adopted her opinions, and were not slow in propagating them. An effort was made to have Wheelwright settled as pastor in Boston, which led to great excitement and serious divisions. Governor Vane, and Cotton, the pastor in Boston, placed themselves on the side of the Hutchinsonians. The General Court met in 1637, and the matter came to a crisis. Vane and those who sympathized with him were in the minority. He was not re-elected governor, but Winthrop, who was orthodox, was elected in his stead. Wheelwright was expelled as "guilty of sedition." The Synod of 1637 declared against the sedition, and Cotton finally came back to the orthodox position, and declared that he "disrelished all these opinions and expressions, as being some of them heretical, some of them blasphemous, some of them erroneous, and all of them incongruous." The respectability of the Hutchinsonian aberration disappeared with the surrender of Cotton, who, as Mather declared, "was not the least part of the country." Mrs. Hutchinson was excommunicated, went to the Rhode Island colony, and united with the co-religionists of Roger Williams. But she had a small following here, and removed farther south, where she was murdered by the Indians.

4. **The Half-way Covenant.**—The first practice of the New England Church was that only persons professing to have faith in Christ, and to have become regenerate, were members of the Church, and had the privilege of having their children baptized. But many of the descendants of the colonists, and many who came over as new members of the colonies, made no profession of experimental faith. What was their position? The parents of such adults were anxious they should be received as members of the Church, and that their children should be baptized. Others declared against such action. Then, again, the law of 1631 maintained those who were not members of the Church could not be political freemen: "No man shall be admitted to the freedom of this body politic but such as are members of some of the churches within the limits of the same." If only those professing experimental religion could belong to the Church, many children could not

be baptized, and many adults could not have political rights. Connecticut was the first scene of this important controversy, but Boston was the place where the matter culminated. The meeting of ministers in Boston in 1657, and the General Synod there in 1662, decided in favor of granting membership in the Church to all who owned in person the covenant made in their behalf by their parents, and led a life "not scandalous," and gave themselves and their children to the Lord. To the children of such persons the rite of baptism should not be denied. This synodal deliverance was called the Half-way Covenant, which produced universal agitation in New England, and was not suppressed until the great revival in the middle of the last century.

5. **The Effect of the Half-way Covenant** was universally disastrous. Persons who now entered the Church could do so on simple acknowledgment of the baptismal covenant and the leading of a moral life. Regeneration was not necessary. Children of the unregenerate could be baptized, and the whole family were then connected with the Church. Repentance might be felt to be important, but, not being made a condition of membership, its value was not considered as great as formerly. The general tendency was a lowering of the spiritual standard of church membership throughout New England.

6. **A New View of the Lord's Supper** was now advanced. It was held that the Lord's Supper was a means of regeneration, and that unconverted persons might safely be admitted to the sacrament of the Lord's Supper. The Brattle Street Church, Boston, was the first to advocate this new doctrine. The Rev. Solomon Stoddard, of Northampton, grandfather of

Jonathan Edwards, publicly defended it, in 1707, in a sermon in which he declared that "sanctification is not a necessary qualification for partaking of the Lord's Supper, and that the Lord's Supper is a converting ordinance." His views were opposed by Increase Mather and others. But Stoddard's theory was the natural consequence of the Half-way Covenant. It found favor in many parts of New England. The effect was to intensify the disastrous tendency of the Half-way Covenant. The churches were greatly increased by the addition of unconverted members. Some of the churches consisted chiefly of unregenerate people. The conditions of repentance and conversion not being required for admission to membership and to the sacred ordinances, there was the same laxity in receiving unconverted candidates into the ministry. Between the years 1680 and 1750 many such persons became preachers, and were settled as pastors. Their sermons were unspiritual, and their parishioners were cold and formal. The outcome of the whole movement was the great Unitarian secession. Cotton Mather's prediction was fulfilled: "Should this declension continue to make progress as it has done, in forty years more convulsions will ensue, and churches will be gathered out of churches."

II.
The National Period.
1783-1800.

Chapter I.
THE CHURCH AT THE FOUNDING OF THE REPUBLIC.

1. The Contrast between the Church in the Old World and in the New, during the one hundred and eighty-six years of the Colonial Period, was marked. The controversies of Protestantism on the Continent, especially in Germany, had a demoralizing effect. The struggle between the Lutherans and the Reformed had thrown the spiritual life into the background, and had given way to the incoming of rationalism from England and France, and thus made the growth of a native German scepticism a lamentable fact. In England the Wesleyan revival was the only salutary force against the alarming Deism. The religious life in America, while it was always more or less disturbed by European impulses, had grown. Now and then there was an interruption. There were abnormal tendencies, such as might be expected in a land where the conditions were new. But the general life had been progressive and salutary. The theological activity, the prevalence of revivals, the building of churches, and the evangelistic spirit, had produced a strong and aggressive type of ecclesiastical life. The colonial founders of the American Church builded wisely, and made the best possible use of the materials at their command.

2. There was a General Spiritual Decline in the religious life of the Church from about 1765 until the end of the eighteenth century. The absorbing topic was the struggle for national independence. All spiritual interests languished. When once the Revolution commenced, it became the passion of the people until it was concluded. Many of the preachers entered the army as chaplains and officers. A large number of congregations were without pastoral care, and were broken up. Some of the churches were converted into hospitals. Money which would have flowed into spiritual channels was turned into the scanty treasury of the colonies for Washington's army. The peaceful Quakers and Mennonites of Pennsylvania forgot their usual attitude, and eagerly enlisted in the army. When peace came, a new ecclesiastical life needed to be built up. At no time in the history of the American Church was the condition so serious. It was a question, how would Christian people now act, with the boon of a nation in their hands? Until the beginning of the nineteenth century it was a doubt whether the national independence would prove a spiritual blessing or a curse.

3. The Sceptical Tendencies from France became a serious threat. The long residence of Franklin in France, the sympathy of Jefferson with Deism, the popular writings of Thomas Paine, and the helpfulness of Lafayette and other Frenchmen in our national struggle had the effect of making French infidelity popular. William and Mary College, Yale

64 THE CHURCH IN THE UNITED STATES.

College, the incipient Unitarianism in Harvard, and certain unfavorable indications in Princeton College made it appear that unless there was some great spiritual movement the country might be overspread with scepticism. There were men who saw the danger, and labored earnestly to avert it. Happily, with the beginning of the new century there was a great revival, which extended over a larger area than any former one. The infidelity of the time was consumed. The churches found all their energies taxed to take proper care of their new adherents and provide schools for the young.

4. **The Numerical Strength** of the Church at the beginning of the National Period was about as follows:

	Ministers.	Churches.
Episcopalians	250	300
Baptists	350	380
Congregationalists	575	700
Presbyterians	140	300
Lutherans	25	60
German Reformed	25	60
Reformed Dutch	25	60
Methodists	24	11
Associate	13	20
Moravians	12	8
Roman Catholics	26	52
Total	1465	1951

There was a decided tendency in several of these bodies to divide on questions of doctrine and polity. It seems to have been a time when the spirit of national independence invaded the ecclesiastical pale. The air was filled with rumors of division. Some of the churches did suffer serious schisms at this time, which have not yet been healed.

CHAPTER II.

THE SEPARATION OF CHURCH AND STATE.

1. The Church had been a Part of the Colonial System.
—The citizen had been taxed for the support of the Church. In Massachusetts Colony only the man who was a member of the Church could hold political office. In Maryland and Virginia and some other Southern colonies the Established Church of England was as fully a part of the system of civil government as in England itself. There was a great variety in the mode of connection between the Church and the colonial government. But the connection was positive and strong. When the Revolution severed the civil bonds with England, a strong tendency towards the separation of the Church from all political government immediately set in. The general conscience demanded that the new republic should leave the largest liberty to the individual judgment. The people insisted on placing the support of the Church, in all its departments, upon the voluntary judgment of the adherents. This assertion of the voluntary principle in ecclesiastical support and government was one of the most original of all the great phenomena of this stage in our national life.

2. Virginia was the scene of the first great movement to carry into practical effect the voluntary principle. To the Baptists belongs the honor of being the herald. They began amid the first excitement of the revolutionary struggle. In 1775, after a struggle of twenty-seven years against the Established Church of Virginia, they presented to the House of Assembly of Virginia a petition "that they might be allowed to worship God in their own way, without interruption; to maintain their own ministers, separate from others; and to be married, buried, etc., without paying the clergy of other denominations." At the first meeting of the Presbytery of Hanover, Virginia, after the commencement of the war, that body presented a lengthy and able petition for religious liberty In their movement they had the co-operation of the Quakers. In 1777 and 1778 the contest between the friends and enemies of the Establishment became still fiercer, and, against the proposal to enjoin a general assessment for the support of all denominations—which seemed very likely to be adopted—the Presbytery of Hanover presented a remonstrance, in which we find this strong language: "As it is contrary to our principles and interest, and, as we think, subversive of religious liberty, we do again most earnestly entreat that our Legislature would never extend any assessment for religious purposes to us, or to the congregations under our care." The proposed assessment was abandoned.

3. Thomas Jefferson, who in matters religious was to all intents and purposes a Frenchman, introduced an act into the Legislature of Virginia in 1785 "for establishing religious freedom." This was adopted, and perfect religious liberty was now brought to pass in the oldest of the colonies. Maryland followed Virginia. Other states adopted similar measures. In New England there was more caution in making the Church separate from the State. The last state to make the Church independent of the civil government was Massachusetts, the separation taking place in 1833.

Chapter III.

REVIVAL AT THE BEGINNING OF THE CENTURY.

1. **The Revival of 1797-1803** had several important centres of operation. The movement began almost simultaneously in widely separated regions, and extended until the intervening spaces were covered by its effects. In Connecticut the spiritual outpouring was very extensive, and from there it extended throughout New England. From 1797 to 1803 not less than one hundred and fifty churches in New England were powerfully quickened, and large numbers were added. In Kentucky and Tennessee there was the same great spiritual demonstration. Here was a strong population of the Scotch-Irish element. But these people were surrounded by many who made no profession of religion, by others who were outspoken sceptics, and others who were given up to gross immorality. Craighead, Gready, Hoge, Burke, and the McGees were leaders in the movement. People assembled on week days for worship in the open air. All denominations united in work. Multitudes were awakened and converted. From this revival the Western Church received an impulse which has continued down to the present time.

2. **The Colleges** shared largely in this revival. Yale had only about a dozen students who professed religion. But there was such a powerful awakening that seventy-five students became Christians, and united with the Church. In Dartmouth and Williams colleges there

were similar awakenings, and large accessions of students to the churches. Many of the young men who were converted afterwards entered the ministry. Of the seventy-five in Yale College who joined the church, about one half became ministers.

3. A Great Impulse towards Evangelization was imparted by this revival. The Western population had been reached as never before, and the Kentucky and Tennessee region was made the starting-point for missionary work farther west. About this time the entire American Church first saw its great opportunity on the frontier. Young men from the Eastern colleges were enthusiastic in their desire to travel into all parts of the West, found churches and schools, and distribute the Bible and religious books. There was a new faith in evangelistic influence. The old prejudice against Whitefield and his methods had long since passed away, and there was a new and general belief in the reality and power of special spiritual manifestation.

4. Other Advantages to the Church grew out of that wonderful work of grace. Besides the large accessions in membership and the great increase in ministerial candidates, an impulse was given to the production and circulation of religious literature. Missions for the neglected population at home, especially among the Indians, were revived or organized anew. The founding of Sunday-schools, tract organizations, and the American Bible Society sprang out of the warm inspiration of this great spiritual ingathering.

Chapter IV.

EXPANSION IN THE SOUTH AND WEST.

1. **The Roman Catholic Pre-occupation** in the West and South gave abundant promise of a permanent population of adherents to that communion. From the head-waters of the Mississippi down to the Gulf, and along the tributary rivers, there had been settlements of the Jesuits, which preserved the Roman Catholic spirit after the most of the missions had been broken up. The Louisiana Purchase from Napoleon Buonaparte, in 1803, designed to replenish his exchequer for carrying on his war with Spain, brought into the Union the states of Louisiana, Mississippi, Alabama, Arkansas, and Missouri. The population was in large part French, with a Spanish admixture, and the Roman Catholic faith predominated everywhere. Florida came into the Union, by cession from Spain in 1819. Here, too, the pre-occupation had been Roman Catholic. There was a universal dearth of Protestant population and spirit. The first Protestant society in St. Louis, for example, was organized as late as 1818. The vices of the Continent, such as Sabbath desecration, prevailed exclusively in this new territory.

2. **The Protestant Current Westward** did not take the shape of a religious movement. It was simply the expansion of the solid and permanent population east of the Alleghanies. Many of the settlers went as small groups, and some of them as individual adventurers.

They built huts, made a clearing, and in due time were joined by others. The population was Protestant, and partook of the national American feeling. Log churches were built, with such ministerial supply as the scanty means afforded. Many settlers went from Virginia and North Carolina into Tennessee and Kentucky. In time this emigration extended across the Mississippi into Arkansas and Missouri. There were large bodies, such as the land companies of the latter half of the last century. Among these were the Ohio Company, the Transylvania Company, and the Mississippi Company. The Western Reserve, in the northern part of Ohio, was filled by families from New England. The churches in the East, and especially the Home Missionary societies, sent out ministerial agents to travel through the new regions, and especially the valley of the Mississippi, who brought home reports of the spiritual destitution, and made successful appeals for its relief.

3. **The Denominations** taking the lead in the great work of Western and Southern evangelization were the Baptists, Presbyterians, and Methodists. The Presbyterians entered Mississippi about 1800, and Indiana about 1805. The Baptists organized work in Illinois in 1796, in Missouri about the same time, in Indiana in 1802, and in Arkansas about 1818. The Methodists entered Indiana in 1802, and Arkansas in 1815. The Baptists and Methodists began in Wisconsin in 1836. Down to 1805 there were no settlements of native Americans in New Orleans. As late as 1801 there were no Christian people in the old town of Detroit, "except a black man who appeared pious." In due time all the larger religious bodies of the East sent ministers into Michigan and other northwestern regions. The Congregationalists were among the first to expose the spiritual

destitution of the great West, and have been among the most heroic in relieving it. The Protestant Episcopal Church, being strong in Virginia and other southern states, extended itself in the Southwest. The Methodists were early in Texas. Their itinerants, however, went over all the new region, and organized their infant societies as a part of the general ecclesiastical system. No denomination can claim the chief honor of this wonderful evangelization in the South and West. The great religious currents moved along the parallels of latitude westward with a steadiness and persistency which belong to the rarer spiritual phenomena of modern times.

4. **The Moral Significance** of the Western and Southern occupation by the Protestants of the United States is great. We are too near the scene, and the time is too recent, to comprehend the vastness of the achievement. Centuries must elapse before the transformation can be seen in all its meaning. The western and southern parts of the field of the American Church are now sources of supply for the East. Let the harvests of the Mississippi valley fail one season, and there is not a church treasury in the land which is not seriously disturbed by it. The churches in the West which needed help thirty years ago have already pushed out their forces to the Pacific, and have helped to develop the coast from Washington down to San Diego. The national life has been saved by the West. Without the Western legions which followed the United States flag in the Civil War, with the devotion of Crusaders, the Union would to-day be only a memory. Our religious literature, the pulpit, our denominational treasuries, have all been enriched beyond calculation by the contributions which the West has made with liberal hand and sublime faith.

Chapter V.

THE LARGER AND EARLIER DENOMINATIONS.

1. The Protestant Episcopal Church.—The founding of the Virginia Colony at Jamestown was the first act towards the establishment of the Church of England in America. Special attention was given to the church services and the support of the clergy. In 1619 the colony was divided into seven parishes. In 1785 the first General Convention of the Protestant Episcopal Church of the United States was held in Philadelphia. Seven states were represented. The Prayer Book ordered by the convention was published in the following year. It showed traces throughout of the liberal spirit of the new Republic. The omissions from the Book of Common Prayer already in use were remarkable. Among them were the Nicene and Athanasian creeds; the descent into hell, of the creed; absolution; and baptismal regeneration. The bishops were made amenable to the lower clergy. The Prayer Book received no favor in England. The bishops were so opposed to it that some of the more important omissions were restored. But absolution in visitation of the sick and the Athanasian Creed were not restored. The Parliament, by a special act, ordered the ordination to the episcopacy of William White, Samuel Provost, and Dr. Griffith, in 1787. The Thirty-nine Articles were ratified in 1832. The Protestant

Episcopal Church has been distinguished for its educated clergy, its steady growth, and liberality.

2. **The Congregationalists** are the direct descendants of the Pilgrims. The Plymouth Colony, colonists who came over in the *Mayflower*, and landed at Plymouth in 1620, established Puritan principles. This colony was rapidly reinforced by the arrival of others. A colony landed at Salem in 1629, and another in Charlestown in 1635. The Cambridge Platform, which contained the doctrinal basis for American Congregationalism, was adopted in 1648. The first teachers, as well as the first preachers to the New England colonists, had been educated in the Cambridge University. The course of study in Harvard was largely theological. The first object was to educate preachers of the gospel, and a general literary education was subsidiary. The first generation of Congregational ministers was distinguished for its learning. John Cotton, Increase Mather, and Cotton Mather gave tone to the whole body of New England clergy. The literary fertility of the times was remarkable. Besides, the Congregational clergy were distinguished for their wise and brave leadership in all national and social questions. This field they have never left. They have been among the strongest and earliest champions for the freedom of the slaves. They are equally distinguished for their literary and theological productions, for the part they have taken in educating the freedmen, and for organizing churches and founding institutions of learning in the newer portions of the West.

3. **The Reformed Church** was established by the Dutch colony on Manhattan Island, in 1623. The first regular preaching was by Machælius, who arrived from Holland in 1628. A close connection with the Church

in Holland was retained during the colonial period. The Dutch language was long preserved in the churches, and the clergy were brought over from the mother country for the prominent pulpits in New York, Albany, and other places. It was not until 1771 that an independent organization of the Church was effected. This was brought about chiefly through the agency of the Rev. Dr. J. H. Livingston. In 1822 a secession took place, under the name of the "True Reformed Dutch Church." The alleged ground was a departure in doctrine and discipline from the original purity of the Church. The theology of the Reformed Church is Calvinistic, and is based on the Confession of Dort and the Heidelberg Catechism. The clergy have always been distinguished for their learning and popular ability, while the membership have been characterized by rare intelligence and purity of life.

4. **The Baptists.**—Roger Williams, after being expelled by the Pilgrims, founded the Baptist Church in America, in 1639. He organized the colony of Rhode Island, which became a refuge for people of various dissenting creeds. Providence was the chief town. Baptists settled along the eastern shore of Maryland and in Virginia, but in the latter colony they were severely persecuted. Rhode Island, Pennsylvania, and Delaware were the only states where they enjoyed religious liberty. When the national independence was achieved, the Baptists grew rapidly in strength and numbers. Their later history has been a steady progress. They are distinguished for zeal and culture. Among the smaller Baptist sects are the Anti-mission, the Free, the Seventh-Day, the Church of God, or Winnebrennarians, the Disciples of Christ, or Campbellites, the Tunkers, and the Mennonites.

5. **The German Reformed Church** arose in connection with the Reformed (Dutch) Church. It was organized in 1741, and was Calvinistic. The connection with the Reformed continued until 1792, when it became a separate organization. Its original members were Germans, who came from Switzerland and the Palatinate, and were attached to the Helvetic Confession and Heidelberg Catechism. The territory where it is most strongly established is Eastern Pennsylvania. Its clergy have been carefully educated, and its authors have taken an honorable place in American theology.

6. **The Lutheran Church.**—There were three Lutheran currents in the colonies. First, the New York current; second, the Swedish current along the Delaware; and, third, the German current of Pennsylvania. The Germans were early settlers in New York, and they established the Lutheran Church shortly after their arrival. Their first pastor was the Rev. Jacob Fabricius (1669), and they built their first church, a log hut, in 1671. Their next settlement was on the Delaware, in 1676. The Rev. H. M. Muhlenberg, who arrived from Germany in 1742, became the leader of the Lutheran Church in the United States. The first Synod was held in 1748.

7. **Pennsylvania and Ohio** are the two states where the Lutherans have been strongest, but their Church is growing rapidly in Illinois, Wisconsin, Missouri, and other states where there is a large German immigration. Three Lutheran schools exist: The strict, or old Lutherans, who adhere to the theology of the Lutheran fathers; the moderate Lutherans of the Pennsylvania Synod, who have undergone variations from the original theology of the Lutherans of Germany; and the Evangelical Lutherans, who are strictly or-

thodox, and derive their theology from Gettysburg. The chief variation of the American Lutherans from their brethren in Germany is in the American opposition to consubstantiation and private confession.

8. **The Presbyterian Church** took its origin from persons of Presbyterian faith who came to the colonies from Scotland and the north of Ireland in the latter part of the seventeenth century. From 1660 to 1685 three thousand emigrants arrived in America, as fugitives from persecution, the most of them settling in Pennsylvania. Some of them settled on the eastern shore of Maryland. Here, near the village of Salisbury, Maryland, the first Presbyterian church in America was built. No toleration was allowed the Presbyterians in New England. The Scotch-Irish element, which has become renowned in the ecclesiastical history of the United States, has contributed such families as the Alexanders, the Duffields, the Hodges, and the Breckenridges to the American Church. The Philadelphia Presbytery was formed in 1706, and the first General Assembly was held in 1789. In 1838 the Presbyterian Church was divided into the New and the Old Schools. In 1870 the two Schools united. No American Church has surpassed the Presbyterian in the culture of its members, the abilities of the clergy, in devotion to education, in zeal for missions, in munificence, and in devotion to its theology.

9. **The Moravian Church** in America arose from the personal visit of Count Zinzendorf in the year 1741. His first attention was directed to the conversion of the Indians in Pennsylvania. A district west of the Delaware became the centre of the work of the Moravians. The towns of Bethlehem and Nazareth were settled by them. They had a flourishing congregation

in Philadelphia, and others in other parts of the country, notably at Salem, North Carolina. The early character of the Moravians for missionary zeal and excellent schools has been well sustained.

10. **The Methodist Episcopal Church** was established in New York in 1776. The first society was organized by Barbara Heck, Philip Embury, and Captain Webb. Richard Boardman and Joseph Pilmore were sent out by John Wesley in 1769, and Francis Asbury and Richard Wright arrived two years later. The first Conference was held in Philadelphia in 1773, when the Church consisted of ten preachers and one thousand one hundred and sixty members. During the Revolutionary War the Methodists made no material progress, and Asbury, suspected of being a Tory, was compelled to live in concealment. The Methodist Episcopal Church divided in 1844 on the question of slavery, the new Church taking the name of the Methodist Episcopal Church, South. In 1866, the centennial celebration was held throughout the Church at home and in the mission fields. Contributions, chiefly for education, were made, amounting to about eight millions of dollars. An Œcumenical Methodist Council was held in London in 1881, where delegates were present from nearly all the branches of the Methodist family.

Chapter VI.

THE SMALLER EVANGELICAL BODIES.

1. The Multiplication of Ecclesiastical Organizations has been one of the characteristics of American religious life. The many sects in the United States have arisen largely from the cosmopolitan character of the immigrant population. The various Protestant countries of Europe which sent their colonists here were themselves divided in their Protestant attachments. It is not surprising, for example, that there should be both Lutherans and Reformed here—for the German Protestants were divided into these two great classes. The seeds of all the larger and of nearly all the smaller bodies in this country are to be found either in well-defined form in the Old World, or in the theology which the colonists and their successors brought with them.

2. The Presbyterian Subdivisions are numerous. The Associate Church arose from a secession from the Church of Scotland in 1733. The seceders founded an Associate Presbytery, which became an important body in Scotland. In less than twenty years after the secession a number of Scotch Presbyterians in Pennsylvania sent over to the Associate Presbytery for ministers, who came and organized the new American Associate Church. By 1801 they had four presbyteries. The Associate Reformed Church was organized in 1782, and the Reformed Presbyterian Church in 1798. All three of these churches have adopted the Calvinistic theology. The Cumberland Presbyterians arose from the great revival of 1800 in the Cumberland Mountains of Kentucky and Tennessee, chiefly through the labors of the Rev. James McGrady. Several young men offered themselves for the ministry; but the Presbyterian Synod of Kentucky refused them ordination, on the ground of their opposition to the doctrine of election in the Westminster Confession. The result was a secession, and the formation in 1810 of the Cumberland Presbyterian Church.

3. **The Baptists have also their Subdivisions.**—The Seventh-Day Baptists have churches in many parts of the country, chiefly in New York, Rhode Island, Ohio, Virginia, and some of the Western States. The Disciples of Christ, or Campbellites, arose from the labors of Dr. Alexander Campbell, about the year 1812. Their chief numerical strength is to be found in Northern Ohio and several of the Western States. The Free (Will) Baptists originated in New Hampshire in 1780, chiefly through the labors of Benjamin Randall. Their principal strength is in Maine and other New England States. The Quakers and Mennonites are Baptists in theology, and are descendants of German and Dutch immigrants to Pennsylvania. There are other Baptist subdivisions, such as the Anti-mission Baptists, the General Baptists, and the Church of God (Winnebrennarians).

4. **The Smaller Methodist Churches** are not less numerous than those of the Baptists and Presbyterians. The Methodist Protestant Church is a secession from the Methodist Episcopal Church, on the ground of objection to Episcopacy. It took organic shape about 1828. The United Brethren in Christ were organized about 1789. Their founders were from the German

Reformed, the Lutherans, and the Mennonites. The Evangelical Association, arising through the labors of the Rev. Jacob Albright, was organized about 1800. The African Methodist Episcopal Church was formally established in 1816. The African Methodist Episcopal Zion Church is of later origin. Both these churches have their chief constituency in the Southern States, among the colored people. The larger Methodist churches of Canada have united, and bear the general name of the Methodist Church of Canada.

Chapter VII.

THE QUAKERS.

The **Friends**, or **Quakers**, arose as a religious body in England about the middle of the seventeenth century. Their founder was George Fox. He visited the American colonies, and established societies in many places. He and his followers avoided controversy, and quietly pursued their course. The laws of all the colonies except Pennsylvania and Maryland were adverse to them. But, driven from one place, they went quietly to another, without murmuring. One of their early advocates in this country was George Keith. He afterwards left the Quakers, and united with the Church of England. The first colony of Quakers was founded in America about 1661; but others followed in quick succession. A powerful impulse was given to this new sect by the example of William Penn, who was the son of an English admiral. Penn was pure and wise, and of remarkable strength of character. His sense of justice was worthy of any Christian age.

Chapter VIII.

THE ROMAN CATHOLIC CHURCH.

1. The First Great Opportunity of Roman Catholicism in the United States was the colonial missions of the French and Spanish along the St. Lawrence and the Lakes, the Mississippi valley, Florida, and the Pacific coast. The Canadian Romanism is the best of all these types. The missions of the Mississippi valley failed, and Protestants began on a soil fully ready for them by virtue of the failure of their Roman Catholic predecessors. The Pacific coast had its chain of missions, which have also failed.

2. The Second Great Opportunity of Roman Catholicism in this country has been successful, namely, the cultivation of the vast Roman Catholic immigration from Ireland and other Catholic countries. In 1790, out of the 3,200,000 of the country, only 30,000 were Roman Catholics. There were but 26 priests. In New York there were but 100 Roman Catholics, and of them only 40 were communicants. There was but one church, St. Peter's, on Barclay Street. There were but 40 Roman Catholics in Boston, and no church until 1803. The Roman Catholic population to-day is about 12,000,000. In 1790 the population was two out of every 220 of the population; now it is two out of every 11. There was not one school in 1790; now they are numbered by the thousand. Instead of one bishop—the estimable Carroll—with his 30 priests, in 1790, there are 13 archbishops, 75 bishops, 8000 priests, 2000 theological students, 7000 churches, and 3000 chapels and stations. With all this great increase there has been an immense loss of Roman Catholic population. Had the Irish immigrants and their immediate descendants remained Catholics, there would now be 15,000,000 Irish Catholics in the United States. But the fact is there are but 7,000,000—a loss of over one half. There is a shrinkage of 2,000,000 in the Catholic immigration from Germany, Italy, and other countries.

3. **The Ecclesiastical Organization** began in 1789, with the consecration and appointment of the Rev. John Carroll as Bishop of the United States. He was a native of Maryland, a devoted patriot, a man universally respected, and in every way adapted to lay the new foundations of the Roman Catholic Church in the United States. He saw the scanty supply of priests, and labored for their multiplication; he gave an impulse to the erection of churches; he developed the growth of religious orders and communities; he sought to reproduce here the European care of the sick and the poor. The spirit which Carroll infused, the strength of his character, and his amazing foresight have entered into the whole subsequent history of Romanism in the United States. The other two great Roman Catholic bishops, who, each in his day, was the leader of his faith in this country—England (1820) and Hughes (1838)—have only followed in the footsteps of the great Carroll. The Jesuits have made the whole United States one vast mission field. They derive their authority directly from Rome.

4. **The Educational System** of the Roman Catholic Church has been compelled to undergo in the New World a modification entirely new in its history. The

laws of the states favored public schools. The Roman Catholics were compelled to send their children to the public schools, or provide schools at their own expense. In New York the effort was made to have their own schools, and to have an appropriation of the public school funds. The first formal effort was made by Bishop Hughes in 1840. This failed, but the Public School Society agreed to eliminate from the text-books such passages as are objectionable to the Roman Catholics, and to have read in the schools only such passages of the Scriptures as are translated in the same way in both the Protestant and Roman Catholic versions. In 1853 the Public School Society of New York ceased to exist, and the Board of Education was established instead. There had been no division of the school fund. Parochial schools, in antagonism to the public schools, were organized in New York and other parts of the country, and the demand was made that the public school fund should be divided in their favor. In 1853 this demand was made in eight states of the Union; but in no case was it granted. At present there are about 2697 parochial schools attended by 537,725 children, the general direction being given to parents to withdraw their children from the public schools throughout the United States. The Plenary Council of 1884 directed that Roman Catholic schools should be maintained by all the parishes in the country, and the priests were directed, under threat of expulsion, to found such schools where extreme poverty did not prevent their support.

Chapter IX.

THE UNITARIAN CHURCH.

1. The Unitarians arose from the conflict between the evangelical and non-evangelical parties within the Congregational Church of New England. When Stoddard, of Northampton, favored the admission of the unregenerate to Church membership and the Lord's Supper, and the right of their children to baptism, the foundation was laid for the large Unitarian defection. The first Unitarian congregation was King's Chapel, Boston. It had been an Episcopal church. The Rev. Mr. Freeman was appointed reader in 1782. He introduced a liturgy into his church, from which the doctrine of the Trinity was omitted. He was refused ordination by the American bishops, but in 1787 he was ordained by his church-wardens. Freeman was the first who preached Unitarianism publicly. The first openly Unitarian book was Ballou's work on "The Atonement," published in 1803. The most notable case of open rupture was the election of Dr. Ware, in 1804, as professor in Harvard College, and the election of Kirkland as president in 1812. In the same year the "Memoir of Lindsay," by Belsham, was published in London, which was the first revelation to Americans of the steady disintegrating force which had long been operating upon the body of New England evangelical theology. The Boston Congregationalists so far went over to the Unitarian fold that only two churches remained firm to the old landmarks. The American Unitarian Association, which is the organic centre of the body, was founded in 1825. The Unitarian churches are bound together by a great variety of theological sentiment. There has never been any basis of faith which has been thoroughly satisfactory. The theological strength of Unitarianism lies in its marvellous power of objection.

2. **William Ellery Channing** was the strongest, most symmetrical, and most gifted character produced by the American Unitarians. His sermon in Baltimore, in 1819, on the ordination of the Rev. Jared Sparks, was powerful in crystallizing Unitarian sentiment. It produced a number of replies from the evangelical clergy, notably Woods of Andover and Miller of Princeton. The greatest strength of Channing lay in his capacity to go beyond his chosen theological field. His power as a theologian was moderate. But when he advocated temperance and human liberty he became a hero of whom the whole country might well be proud.

3. **The Literary Spirit** of the Unitarians has always been very prominent. Harvard College passed into their control. They early began to cultivate the literature of the Continent, and to introduce its better productions into this country. Their chief writers have exerted a strong influence on the young American mind. Their literary criticism, their unswerving sympathy with the cause of the slave, and their rapid reflection of the advanced thought of Europe, have given to their writings a hearing and respect well worthy of the genius which produced them.

Chapter X.

THE TRANSCENDENTALISTS.

1. **Transcendentalism,** as an intellectual movement, is one of the minor outgrowths of the Unitarian reaction. It regards knowledge as not limited to things ascertained by the senses, but going beyond them and numbering among its ascertained things such ideas as are claimed to be taught by the intuitions. The letter of the Scriptures, therefore, is not sufficient to satisfy the transcendentalist. His larger book is the leaves of his innate self. He thinks, and what he thinks becomes his chief guide. The Transcendental Club of Boston had its first meeting in 1836, and from that time had a marked effect on the aspiring literary mind of New England.

2. **Theodore Parker** appeared before the public in 1837 as a Unitarian pastor in West Roxbury. After 1848 he ceased to be regarded as even a Unitarian. He had drifted far out of the conservative limits of the Channing School, and was an open assailant of the inspiration of the Scriptures, the divinity of Christ, and, indeed, of the divine framework of the Christian religion. He had studied in Germany during the domination of German rationalism, and brought over to America the anti-scriptural influences which he there absorbed. His violence of language, his want of respect for the phenomena of Christianity, and his defence of the most destructive criticism of the German rationalists, threw him out of the limits of all conservative

minds. His words were sword-strokes. He was as fearless in his declarations against the crime of slavery as a Crusader in his march against the Saracen. He had no system. His writings are varied. He proves but little, though he asserts much. Theology, humane pleadings, literary criticism, are combined in strange mixture. He was a man of large heart, of tender sympathies, and as he approached the end, in Florence, whither he had gone for his health, a reverence and calmness came over him as a breath of peace and gentleness from the Crucified.

3. **Ralph Waldo Emerson** stands easily at the head of the transcendental column. He had drunk in the old New England theology from ancestral days. For eight generations his family had been preachers. In 1830 he became pastor of the Second Church in Boston. But in 1831 he ceased his pastoral care, and henceforth became a writer and a lecturer. He lived without a theological system, and died without a following. With a warm poetic sympathy, with a tender regard for the slave and all in need, and with a gentleness of spirit worthy of Epictetus, he passed through a long career of authorship and observation. All men were his friends, because he was the friend of all. His literary method explains his want of coherence. He put his thoughts, as they came to him, in scrap-books. His writings present all the characteristics of disjunction. His theology and philosophy lay in his supreme faith in the majesty of the intuitions. To the written word of Scripture he gave but little weight. He was Carlyle's great American admirer and interpreter, but without Carlyle's orthodox quality. He is a man to admire, because of his noble qualities of heart and the brightness of his genius. His placid personal life is a beautiful picture. One cannot contemplate it without admiring it.

Chapter XI.

UNIVERSALISTS AND OTHER SMALLER BODIES.

1. **The Universalists** hold the doctrine of universal salvation. They first appeared in New England, about the middle of the eighteenth century. The most prominent apostle of the doctrine was the Rev. John Murray, who came to this country from England in 1770. The Rev. E. Winchester united with them. A third advocate, the Rev. Hosea Ballou, gave increased strength to the movement about 1790. The General Convention of 1803 adopted a basis of faith—the Holy Scriptures as a revelation of the divine character and human duty and destiny; one God, revealed in Jesus Christ, by one Holy Spirit, who will restore the world to holiness and happiness; holiness and happiness are connected; believers ought to practise good works, for they are good and profitable to men. There is variety of view as to the time when final happiness of the unrighteous takes place.

2. **The Swedenborgians** began their organization with the preaching of the doctrines of Swedenborg, or The Church of the New Jerusalem, in Philadelphia, by the Rev. James Glen. In Boston, Samuel Worcester was active in propagating Swedenborgian views, about 1817. The General Convention was organized in 1818. The congregations are chiefly in New England, Ohio, and Pennsylvania. There is a large measure of independent views in the separate congregations. The

theology in one may differ considerably from that of another.

3. **The Shakers** in America owe their origin to James Wardley, who had been a Quaker, but separated from that body. He began to preach the extravagant and superstitious notions which underlie the Shaker system. The great exponent of Shakerism was Ann Lee, who married a man named Standley, and came to this country in 1774. She preached gross extravagances, and called herself "Ann the Word." The Shakers called themselves the Millennial Church, and established themselves as a community at Watervliet, near Albany. They believe in physical contortions as manifestations of spiritual power; that the millennium has already begun; that they have apostolic gifts; that baptism and the Lord's Supper ceased with the apostolic age; and that the judgment has already commenced. Of their history, they thus sing:

> "Hail, thou victorious gospel!
> And that auspicious day,
> When Mother safely landed
> In Hudson's lovely bay;
> Near Albany they settled,
> And waited for a while,
> Until a mighty shaking
> Made all the desert smile."

4. **The Christians** are of threefold origin—Methodist, Baptist, and Presbyterian. The Rev. James O'Kelley, in 1793, withdrew from the Methodist Episcopal Church in North Carolina, on account of objections to the polity of that Church. His views of the Trinity underwent a change about the same time, and he and his followers called themselves Republican Methodists. About ten years later, Dr. Abner Jones, of Vermont, and the Rev. Elias Smith, of New Hamp-

shire, withdrew from the Baptist Church. They were followed by other Baptists in New England and in other states, the basis of their movement being an opposition to all creeds. About the same time the Rev. B. W. Stone, of Kentucky, with others, withdrew from the Presbyterian Church, and called themselves "Christians." These three movements, being in the main alike, amalgamated, and took the general name of "Christians." The Christians do not admit the deity of the Holy Ghost or of Christ, at the same time calling Christ "the only-begotten Son of God." They have no general unity of doctrine, their main bond being an opposition to all creeds. They have exerted no general influence on the life of the country.

5. **The Rappists and Others.**—In 1803 George Rapp came over to the United States from Germany, bringing with him a small colony. The colonists settled at Economy, near Pittsburgh, where they established themselves. They then went to Indiana, but afterwards returned to Economy, where they have remained to the present time. The *Hicksite Quakers* arose from Elias Hicks, a Friend, in 1827. They reject the doctrine of the Trinity. The *Millerite* movement was under the leadership of William Miller, who in 1831 proclaimed the second advent of Christ. He was joined by others, who held camp-meetings and revival services, and published several journals and special appeals, in New England and New York. They fixed on April 23, 1843, and other dates, for the destruction of the world, but, the prophecies failing, the most of the Millerites became discouraged, and drifted into different forms of scepticism and superstitition.

Chapter XII.

THE MORMON ABOMINATION.

1. The Mormon Antecedents are not admirable. To Vermont belongs the responsibility of producing the two great Mormon leaders, Joseph Smith and Brigham Young. The beginnings of the Mormon system are so ridiculous, so enveloped in either superstition or gross imposture, that they merit universal contempt. Joseph Smith, the first apostle, claimed to be the author of the "Book of Mormon," published in Palmyra, New York, in 1830. Sidney Rigdon had become a Mormon preacher and joined Smith the year before. In 1830 the first church was organized in Manchester, New York. The leaders claimed miraculous powers. In 1831 the whole body removed to Kirtland, Ohio, where they established a colony and built a temple. Brigham Young joined them in 1832, and in 1835 became one of the twelve apostles. The bank which they had founded now failing, the colony removed to Missouri, and then to Nauvoo, Illinois, and finally, in 1845, to Utah.

2. The Origin of the Book of Mormon seems to have been a piece of literary trickery. Solomon Spalding, a Dartmouth graduate, was at one time a minister of the gospel, but retired from the ministry, and removed to Pittsburgh, Pennsylvania, in 1812. He died four years later. His tastes were antiquarian. He studied the mounds of Eastern Ohio, and conceived the idea of writing a book, claiming to be the work of a mound-builder, and to have been found in an ancient mound. He called his fiction, "Manuscript Found," but died before its publication. In 1812 he placed his manuscript in a Pittsburgh printing-office, with which Sidney Rigdon was connected. This man copied it, and returned the manuscript to Spalding, whose death occurred soon afterwards. This book was changed so as to admit the doctrine of the new sect. In lack of a Bible which favored their views, the Mormons patched up Spalding's "Manuscript Found" to such an extent that, under the title of the "Book of Mormon," it became the basis of their creed and the fountain of their abominations. In all literary history no greater train of social corruption has ever followed a piece of literary imposture. It has been translated into many modern languages, and is made the book of final appeal by all Mormons.

3. The Growth of the Mormon Body is largely due to the great immigration of its dupes from England, Scandinavia, and other parts of Europe. In 1837 Orson Hyde and H. C. Kimball went to England as missionaries, and succeeded in persuading a number to come to this country and unite their fortunes with the Mormons. Missionaries have been going to Europe ever since, and have induced many to come to America and become Mormons. In their missionary appeals to the European peasantry they hold out the inducement of a home and property. To unsuspecting and uneducated persons, who have long been looking to America as their home, and have been kept at home for the want of passage money, the offer to pay all expenses to Utah has been too flattering to be resisted. The illusion is kept up until their arrival. From Utah the Mormons

have extended into New Mexico, Arizona, Montana, Idaho, and Wyoming. They are generally good farmers, and have developed much territory which they have brought to great fruitfulness. The alleged Mormon population is 138,000, which is probably far beneath the actual number.

4. **The Edmunds Law**, prohibiting polygamy and imprisoning all men guilty of it, has been the first successful step to establish the laws of the United States over this abnormal community. With the legal proscription of polygamy it is likely that the crime will become less a part of the Mormon system. Probably the Mormons will in due time formally throw overboard that one cardinal feature and retain the rest. They know how to adapt themselves to circumstances. The Mormons prosper chiefly by raising the cry of persecution.

5. **The Antidote to Mormonism** has been provided. Various evangelical bodies have sent their missionaries to Utah, who labor in the midst of that Mormon stronghold. The first missionary to Salt Lake was a Congregationalist, the Rev. Norman McLeod, in 1864. The Episcopalians, the Presbyterians, and the Methodists followed in rapid succession. The method of work has been to establish services and found schools. There are now about three hundred preachers and teachers engaged in the gigantic undertaking of uprooting Mormonism. Their work is difficult, but the recent advance has been decided. No part of our country makes stronger appeal than this for money and for workers. No one who goes into a distant land to combat heathenism has a more difficult task than he has who settles down among the Mormons, and sets up the banner of the cross with a view to eradicate the most glaring, disloyal, and corrupt monstrosity which has ever inflicted itself upon our American civilization.

Chapter XIII.

THE ANTI-SLAVERY REFORM.

1. American Slavery was the outgrowth of European cupidity. In 1619 a Dutch frigate stopped at Jamestown, Va., and sold fourteen negroes to the colonists. Others were brought afterwards, and sold at various times during the century. By the year 1670 there were two thousand slaves in Virginia. But this colony did not stand alone. Slavery existed in all the colonies. Newport, R. I., was the American centre of the slave trade with the West Indies and Africa. It was the custom to make slaves of the Indians captured in war.

2. The Colonial Protest against slavery became very decided as the number of slaves increased and gave signs of becoming a permanent institution. No strong voice was raised in justification of the system. It seems to have been always regarded as an evil—an unfortunate necessity growing out of the colonial need of labor. But many opposed its growth, and lifted their voice against the condition of the slaves. By the year 1700 there was a strong sentiment throughout New England against it. John Eliot, the apostle to the Indians, in 1675 presented a memorial to the Governor and Council of Massachusetts against selling captured Indians into slavery, and against the wretched condition of the enslaved Africans. The Quakers of Philadelphia presented to their Yearly Meeting, in 1688, a strong protest against "buying, selling, and holding men in slavery." All Quakers stood boldly against the sin, and declared that it ought to be crushed. William Penn's "concern for the souls of the blacks" pervaded the entire body of his co-religionists. John Wesley, while a missionary in Georgia, protested against slavery.

3. **The Opposition to Slavery** at the time of the national independence was universal. It was considered, as in the earlier period, a great misfortune, which ought to be removed at the earliest possible moment. In Virginia its abolition was publicly advocated. In Tennessee and Kentucky the public press waged a bitter warfare for its extermination. Pennsylvania was the centre of the crusade. The Pennsylvania Abolition Society, organized before the Revolution, was re-established in 1784. Franklin, Benezet, Rush, Hopkins, and others labored earnestly for the arrest and extirpation of slavery. All the great Revolutionary leaders — Washington, Adams, Jefferson, Hamilton, Jay, and the rest—stood as a unit against it. In addition to Pennsylvania, other states had their abolition societies—that of New York being organized in 1785, Rhode Island in 1789, Connecticut in 1790, and New Jersey in 1792.

4. **All the Churches** took the same view of the sin of slavery. Elias Neare, of New York, labored from 1704 to 1708 for the conversion and instruction of the negroes in that city. In Virginia it was considered proper that the negroes should be instructed, and measures were adopted for that end. John Wesley sent over to the Rev. Mr. Davis, of Virginia, books for the benefit of the colored people in that clergyman's needy parish. An important literature against slavery sprang up. Anti-slavery writings of the Old

World found a ready sale in the New. John Wesley's "Thoughts on Slavery" was republished here, and found many readers throughout the colonies. Slavery had, as yet, no strong apologist.

5. **The Quiescent Period** extended from about 1800 to 1830. A general sentiment of indifference prevailed. In the South there were so many slaves, and they seemed to contribute so largely to the material progress of that section, that the system was regarded as a necessity. In the North the agitation was not carried on with the former activity. No plan was proposed which assumed the shape of practical possibility. The most feasible plan seemed to be the deportation of slaves to Africa. The American Colonization Society organized the colony of Liberia, on the west coast of Africa, in 1817, and many humane men advocated the scheme. But the chief service of this worthy institution was to create sympathy with the negroes. As to making Africa a home for the American negroes, in due time the plan was proved to be impracticable. The African negro, though at first an unwilling guest in America, nevertheless likes his home too well to think of leaving it, except to aid in the evangelization of Africa. The war with Mexico, in 1847, resulted in the large accession of Texas as slave territory. Efforts were made to make Kansas a slave state. The public mind became aroused to great excitement on both sides. The political parties took up the question with avidity. The firm friends of the liberation of the slave triumphed in Kansas, and it was admitted as a free state. John Brown, who had led in the movement in Kansas, began a liberating movement in Virginia, where he was arrested and hung as a fomenter of insurrection.

6. **The Emancipation of the Slaves** during the Civil War, by the act of President Lincoln, sustained by the Union armies and the general sentiment of the Northern States, put an end to the long struggle in behalf of the freedom of the slave. The question once in politics, it remained there until settled by the sword. Boston was the centre of the agitation in the North. Anti-slavery movements were conducted in different sections of the country. Benjamin Lundy labored in Western Virginia, from 1815 to 1830, by speech and pen. The Rev. J. Dickey, of Kentucky, about 1824, was engaged in the same work. William Lloyd Garrison began in Vermont the publication of his *Journal of the Times*, in 1828. Boston became, later, his great field of agitation. Gerritt Smith, Joshua Leavitt, G. B. Cheever, Lyman Beecher, A. A. Phelps, Oliver Johnson, Theodore Parker, H. W. Beecher, and Wendell Phillips are only a few of the great names which illuminate the pages of the history of the anti-slavery struggle as it approached its culmination. Whittier has been the great minstrel to reflect in verse the aspiration of the slave for freedom.

7. **The Present Condition** of the liberated slaves and their children is one of the most serious questions for the American Church to solve. The four millions of liberated slaves have grown into seven millions. The churches of the North have organized important measures for their education, which are constantly increasing. There is a universal acquiescence in the extinction of slavery. The South itself regards it as a providential deliverance. Slavery always was a national expense.

Chapter XIV.

THE TEMPERANCE REFORM.

1. **Intemperance during the Colonial Period** was a common vice. It was a heritage from the Old World. Public opinion, even in the clergy, was seriously directed towards its extirpation. It was regarded an evil which might in time be removed. But the day seemed remote, and the manner of the solution of the great question was a problem too deep to engage serious thought. Moderate drinking was common to all classes. The time for enriching the coffers of the producer by chemical admixtures to alcohol had not yet come. The colonial tippler was at least safe in drinking unadulterated liquors. But no man who lives by an unholy traffic remains satisfied without lessening his expense in producing his ware. We are now in the midst of the reign of poisonous compounds. That the evil of intemperance was known and recognized in the colonial times may be seen in a resolution of the first Congress (1774): "Resolved, that it be recommended to the several legislatures immediately to pass laws the more effectually to put a stop to the pernicious practice of distilling, from which the most extensive evils are likely to be derived, if not quickly prevented." This was bold and fearless action. No Congress since then has had the moral courage to pass a like motion.

2. **Early Leaders in the Temperance Reform** were not wanting. The Quakers were a unit in support of it.

The Methodist Episcopal Conference of 1783 asked this question: "Should our friends be permitted to make spirituous liquors, sell and drink them in drams?" To this it gave answer: "By no means: we think it wrong in its nature and consequences; and desire all our preachers to teach the people, by precept and example, to put away this evil." The Presbyterian General Assembly of 1811 made a similarly strong declaration against intemperance. The Congregationalists took equally strong action in the same year. Dr. Rush's book, "The Effects of Ardent Spirits on the Human Mind and Body," published in Philadelphia in 1785, was one of the first American works to prove the deleterious physical and mental effects of alcoholic liquors. It was widely circulated, and exerted a great influence in directing public attention to the growth of intemperance and in organizing measures for its suppression. Jeremy Belknap, of New Hampshire, was a strenuous advocate in the same good cause.

3. **Organizations** for the eradication of intemperance began to be formed shortly after the national independence. The first temperance organization was formed by about two hundred farmers of Connecticut in the year 1789. In 1811 the Massachusetts Society for the Suppression of Intemperance was founded. This society had the support of the strongest men of all denominations in New England. Societies modelled after this one multiplied in various parts of the country, but chiefly in New England. The Washingtonian movement, beginning in 1840, required a pledge of total abstinence. Multitudes gave it their cordial support, and many intemperate people were reclaimed throughout the country. But the interest soon declined. Other associations arose. The National Tem-

perance Society has been a powerful organization for the diffusion of temperance literature and the organization of temperance movements throughout the country. The Roman Catholic Total Abstinence Society, established in 1870, has exerted a powerful influence in continuing in this country the movement begun by Father Matthew in Ireland. The most aggressive of all the associations in this country has been the Woman's Christian Temperance Union, which began with the Woman's Crusade in Ohio in 1874. The president of this association is Miss Frances E. Willard.

4. Constitutional Prohibition is the latest and most radical method of suppressing intemperance in the United States. Maine was the first state to prohibit the manufacture and sale of all intoxicants. Kansas and Iowa followed in the same path. Rhode Island adopted the amendment, but there was never any disposition on the part of the officers to carry it out. By shrewd political management the amendment has been reversed, and now, in the state made immortal by the career of Roger Williams, the saloon has full liberty of destruction. Michigan, Pennsylvania, Kentucky, Texas, and several other states have rejected the amendment by a popular vote. The manufacturers of intoxicating liquor have bent their energies against constitutional prohibition in every state where the question has been submitted to the popular decision.

5. The Friends of the Saloon have spent money with a lavish hand, have subsidized the press, have employed voluble speakers, have misrepresented the operation of the prohibitory laws in states where the constitutional amendment prevails, have presented the bribe of political support to men who will oppose prohibition, and have offered the tempting snare of supporting high license.

Many friends of temperance look upon local option as the best remedy for intemperance. In the Southern States it is the favorite remedy. But this is merely temporary. The territory where liquors are prohibited can easily be reached by the stealthy arm of the vendor from the adjoining territory where it is free. Frequent elections make local option a dream rather than a permanent possession. Many friends of temperance look upon high license as the best method of restriction. This delusion may prevail for a time. A sin is no less a sin because the doer offers a large price for the privilege of committing it. He whose itching palm takes the price is no less a sinner even though the impersonal offender bears the great name of the United States.

Chapter XV.

PHILANTHROPY AND CHRISTIAN UNION.

1. **The Philanthropic Spirit** is one of the most notable of all the developments of the American Church. The early introduction of the voluntary principle as the basis of financial support has become a prominent factor in the growth of the philanthropic spirit. The needs of the Church have required the voluntary gifts of the people. The United States have really done but little, compared with the wealth at command, for the larger humane work of the country. The vast asylums for all the helpless classes have, for the most part, grown out of the spirit of beneficence in the individual citizen. The first gifts of the colonists were for education. These were humble and small, but they were the foundation of that immense giving for educational purposes which has placed the American Church far beyond the Church in other countries.

2. **The Education of the Freedmen** has been recognized as one of the most urgent benevolent causes of the last thirty years. All the larger ecclesiastical bodies have poured down into the Southern country vast sums of money for the education of both the white and colored people. The Peabody Fund, founded by the late George Peabody, has been a source of great help. The Slater fund is every year extending its beneficent work. The general government took the freedmen under its own care at first, by establishing the Freedmen's Bureau.

But this did not meet the want. The churches came in and took its place, and have carried the work far beyond the limits which the government had designed. The Fisk University, in Nashville, is a notable type of an institution founded by Northern beneficence for the education of the colored people in the South. The Vanderbilt University, founded by the late Cornelius Vanderbilt, of New York, is a type of the beneficent spirit of the North operating for the benefit of the whites in the South. These are, however, only portions of the immense sums and the large educational institutions which the South owes to the benevolent spirit of Northern citizens. Beyond all calculation is the power of these golden threads of fraternal love to heal the divisions engendered by the War for the Union.

3. The Treatment of the Indians by the United States is one of the darkest chapters in our national history. The military spirit has predominated in the national management of the aborigines, and the general judgment has been "the only good Indian is the dead Indian." We have crowded the Indians into reservations, and then managed to deprive them again of these. The dealings with the Indians have been managed on the basis of might giving right. The only relief to the dark picture of the government's management of the Indian problem has been the humane policy of the churches. All the early colonial legislation was friendly. The king's instruction to the first colony—Virginia—was: "To provide that the true word and service of God be preached, planted, and used, not only in the said colony, but also as much as might be among the savages bordering upon them, according to the rites and doctrines of the Church of England." Whether by the authority of the original charters, or the voluntary legislation of the colonial governments, the Indian was treated well. The point made by Roger Williams, that the Indian was the real owner of the soil, thoroughly pervaded the better colonists all along the seaboard. But our later treatment has been in antagonism to all our colonial antecedents. The seal of Massachusetts Colony had as its device the figure of an Indian, with the Macedonian cry, "Come over and help us." We have "come over," and cheated and killed. Our wars with the Indians have arisen from Indian depredations produced by the Indian's knowledge that he had been treated unjustly. The wars have been crimes, as fully so as the partition of Poland by Prussia, Austria, and Russia.

4. **Christian Union** has been one of the most beautiful phases of our American ecclesiastical life. Until about 1860 the controversial spirit asserted itself. The Unitarian controversy in New England, and the long conflict between the Calvinistic and Arminian types of theology, pervaded the Northern churches, and reached some parts of the South. But the spirit of ecclesiastical fraternity and wise co-operation now became prominent, due in large measure to the great revival of 1857–59. There had already been beginnings. The Evangelical Alliance, which was founded in 1846, has been a powerful agency in bringing the evangelical churches of the United States into close relationship. The Young Men's Christian Association, founded in 1851 after the model of the London Society for Improving the Spiritual Condition of Young Men engaged in the Drapery and other Trades, in 1844, has brought together a great number of active men for earnest work in caring for young men in every part of the United States. There are now about three thou-

sand branches of this association throughout the world. The Sanitary Commission, a voluntary association for the care of the wounded and suffering during the Civil War, was purely secular, but comprised voluntary workers from many communions. The Christian Commission, also voluntary, consisted of persons who combined Christian sympathy with physical care of the suffering during the war. About twelve million dollars were contributed voluntarily by the people of the North for the carrying on of the work of these two branches of united Christian work.

5. **Christian Co-operation** is constantly advancing. In city missionary work, in societies of young people for Scriptural instruction, in the larger place assigned to the laity in evangelistic effort, one can easily see how rapidly the spirit of unity in work is increasing in every part of the American Church. The present danger is, that many will forget their denominational attachments, and think that any one religious body which furnishes the first field of work is as good as any other.

Chapter XVI.

MISSIONS.

1. The Missionary Spirit of the American Church has been prominent ever since the beginning of the present century. The great revival at that time began early to take the form of an intense activity in behalf of the unevangelized. The expansion of our population in the West revealed such widespread wants in great regions of the country that it seemed as if the demand made upon the Church was far greater than could be supplied. But the heroism displayed by individuals, representing the leading evangelical churches, soon put at rest all misgivings as to the power of the Christian people of the land to extend the blessings of the gospel to every part of the national domain.

2. Missions to the Indians were among the first to receive attention. In 1840 there were about one million eight hundred thousand Indians in the United States and Canada. Seventy thousand of these were half civilized, or in such close relation to our white population as to be under Christian influence. Among some of these tribes the churches sent missionaries, established schools, and published books in the Indian languages. Occasionally an Indian preacher of great popular ability visited the churches in the East, addressed popular audiences, and secured a greatly increased interest in behalf of the spiritual condition of his people. There were two influences at work in relation to the Indians—

the hostile attitude of the general government, which regarded the Indians as an expensive incubus on the nation; and the sympathy of the churches, which regarded the Indians as worthy of spiritual care. The process of decrease of the Indians went steadily on. Their languages became fewer, some being spoken by such decreasing numbers as almost to disappear. The American Bible Society published the Scriptures in a number of the Indian languages, while some of the churches published catechisms, hymns, and other practical books. The churches were in advance of the Bible Society as to time. Some of the parts of the Scriptures, as John's gospel in Mohawk, were published by individual churches.

3. **Home Missions.** — The foreign populations have presented a difficult problem. Thus far only a scanty provision has been made to reach their wants. The Germans, French, Scandinavians, Poles, and other immigrants are still receiving but slight attention compared with the great need. The first Home Missionary Society was organized by the Congregationalists in Connecticut in 1774. The Presbyterians of New York and New Jersey followed in 1789 and 1796, and the Congregationalists of Massachusetts organized the Massachusetts Home Missionary Society in 1799. The polity of the Methodist Episcopal Church requiring an itinerant ministry, the labors of many of its preachers were purely missionary, without the name. The Western field was one great territory for home missionary work. The Methodist Episcopal Missionary Society was organized in 1819, but its labors for the first thirteen years were confined entirely to the home work. All the churches exhibited a profound interest in missionary work. The Protestant Episcopal Church organ-

ized its Board of Missions, for both foreign and home work, in 1820; the Baptists organized their Home Missionary Society in 1832. Some of the churches have Women's Home Missionary Societies which supplement, in a wise and successful way, the regular work of the churches with which they are connected. The field which these latter societies have chosen has been chiefly in the South, on the frontier, and especially in Utah.

4. **The Foreign Field for American Missions** is very broad. From the time when the American Board of Commissioners of Foreign Missions sent out their first group of missionaries — Judson, Newell, and their wives—to India, in 1812, there has been a constant advance in missionary interest in all the churches. The field is now very broad. There are five separate parts: the Protestant countries of the Continent, the Roman Catholic countries, the Greek Catholic countries, the Mohammedan countries, and the Heathen countries. Scandinavia, Germany, Switzerland, and Italy have become special fields. Bulgaria and Turkey, with Constantinople as the centre, have received great attention.

5. **Robert College**, founded on the bank of the Bosphorus by the late Christopher Robert, has been a powerful agent in Christian education for the polyglot population of Turkey. Greece, Syria, Egypt, and the coast of Asia Minor have shared in the beneficent labors of American missions. Missionaries have gone eastward from Turkey as far as the valley of the Tigris and Euphrates, and have almost touched the great band of workers in India. India is one great network of Christian missions, many being organized and supported by the churches of the United States. Already

a vast native Christian population has been developed, with native preachers, teachers, and medical helpers. Burma, with Judson as the great apostle, has become a prosperous field. In Singapore there are American missions and schools. Up the China coast there are others, while all over the eastern part of China, and now in Japan and Korea, men and women from America are preaching, teaching, gathering in orphans, and founding schools. The gospel in the Sandwich Islands is a special triumph of American Christianity. Alaska, our latest northwestern possession, is now becoming a prosperous missionary field. The honor of seeing its importance, and being the first to cultivate this field, belongs to the Presbyterian Church of the United States.

6. The New Africa.—The latest phase in African evangelization is to be found in the opening for the gospel in the regions explored by the immortal David Livingstone. Stanley, with the view of aiding the project of the king of Belgium in founding the Congo Free State, by his travels and the interest awakened by his books describing them, has contributed greatly to the interest in the New Africa on the part of the whole Christian world. Many of the leading churches have already established missions along the Congo. Bishop William Taylor, though now advanced in years, is at work in that newly opened region with all the enthusiasm which marked his earlier labors in California, Australia, South Africa, South America, and India.

Chapter XVII.

CHRISTIAN LITERATURE.

1. The First Publications of the Colonial Writers were largely religious. Even such works as Morton's "Memorial," which was designed to describe the early history of the Plymouth Colony, dealt much in religious matter. Such accounts as were sent back to England, describing the colonial history, gave so much prominence to ecclesiastical and religious matters that one would suppose the writers were dealing with the annals of a church rather than of a colony. The writers, however, were for the most part preachers, and often learned theologians, and the matter which they furnished was welcome to the whole Protestant world of Europe. Eliot's Indian Bible, while it could not be read by an individual in Europe, and by very few in the colonies, aroused a profound foreign interest in American ecclesiastical life. The colleges of Harvard and Yale were centres of a Christian literature. The professors were mostly preachers, and many of the young men who studied under them went into the New England pulpits, and themselves became valuable contributors to the new religious literature of the colonies.

2. Elementary Religious Works were produced at an early period. The "New England Primer," during the eighteenth century, was the little manual which was regarded in New England as necessary for every child's instruction. The catechism prepared by Richard Mather and John Cotton, entitled "Spiritual Milk for Babes," appeared in many forms and for many years, and was incorporated in the "New England Primer" of later date. It was made a part of a primer for the colony of Connecticut, and published about 1715. The "New England Primer" absorbed the necessary parts of other elementary works, and was published in the various colonies. It was edited by many competent hands, and adapted itself to the political changes of the colonies. At one time it was strongly anti-Catholic. It was loyal to the British king, when it was necessary so to be. But in due time it produced Washington's portrait as its frontispiece. The "New England Primer Improved" was the later and final form. It contained hymns by Watts, easy spelling and reading lessons, prayers, acrostics, the Shorter Catechism, and the celebrated "Dialogue between Christ, Youth, and the Devil." The picture of John Rogers at the stake, surrounded by his wife and children, was always a necessary illustration. The couplets, beginning with

"In Adam's fall
We sinned all,"

and closing with

"Zaccheus he
Did climb the tree
His Lord to see,"

were never omitted, as needful exposition of the truth to accompany the quaint illustrations. The "Psalterium Americanum," edited by Cotton Mather, was used for worship extensively. The "Whole Book of Psalms," published in 1640, a literal reprint of the received version, was as near an approach to the Psalter of the Established Church as the prejudices of the Puritan fathers would allow. The great basis of the New England faith was the Westminster Catechism. It was the universal guide. Every pastor went according to it in the colonial period. It was regarded as the great modern triumph of Christianity in Europe. Sermons were preached upon it, and books were published in exposition of it. Samuel Willard, for example, covered a space of nineteen years, by delivering two hundred and fifty lectures on the Shorter Catechism. His works were published after his death in a ponderous volume—the first folio produced by the American press. Sermons were a favorite form of religious literature. Watts's "Psalms and Hymns" went through numerous editions. Religious biography, such as the "Journal of Whitefield," and others, was in general demand. Reprints of Baxter's practical works were common. Only a short time elapsed before a good practical work in England found its way to Boston, and came out from the press of Kneeland, Bumstead, or some other printer of that place. The fruits of the colonial press now appear exceedingly primitive, but they formed an essential part of the religious foundation of the country, and prove to us the early determination of the colonists to develop a religious literature of their own.

3. **The Periodical Religious Press.**—In no country has the religious press so prominent a place as in the United States. The first religious periodical was Thomas Prince's *Christian History*, published in Boston. As with all other departments of Christian activity at the beginning of the nineteenth century, so to the publication of religious periodicals a remarkable impulse was given. The Connecticut *Evangelical Magazine*

began in 1800, the Massachusetts *Missionary Magazine* in 1803, and the *Panoplist* (Boston) in 1805. Others followed in rapid succession. While religious monthlies were the first which came into use, in a short time there were religious weeklies. The Boston *Recorder*, established by the Congregationalists in 1816, was the first. In due time all the various religious bodies had their organs. After a while special religious interests were represented by periodicals, such as Tract and other societies. Many Sunday-school publications are now of periodical character, and great pains are taken to present in them the very latest and best productions of the Christian thought of both Europe and America. Most of the very best theology we have now appears in the religious periodicals of the United States. Researches in Christian archæology and the history of the Church are represented by special periodicals.

4. **Christian Hymnology** has been cultivated by Americans with no little interest and success. Even in the colonial times the rigors of the New England climate and the general privations which the new settlers had to contend with did not prevent the production of devotional hymns. There was a severity in the theology which has not been reproduced for a century or more, but the spirit of real poesy was not wanting. Wigglesworth's "Day of Doom" was a vigorous statement of Christian doctrine in verse. But the golden age of American hymnology has been since the beginning of the national period. Among the most notable hymns produced in this country, and now sung by Christian congregations in many parts of the world, may be mentioned the following:

Timothy Dwight:

"I love thy kingdom, Lord;"

W. B. Tappan:
>"There is an hour of peaceful rest;"

and
>"'Tis midnight; and on Olive's brow;"

Bishop A. Cleveland Coxe:
>"O where are kings and empires now?"

Thomas Hastings:
>"How tender is thy hand;"

John Pierpont:
>"O Thou to whom in ancient times;"

William Hunter:
>"My heavenly home is bright and fair;"

Henry Ware, Jr.:
>"Lift your glad voices in triumph on high;"

George P. Morris:
>"Man dieth and wasteth away;"

Nathaniel P. Willis:
>"The perfect world, by Adam trod;"

Mrs. Lydia H. Sigourney:
>"Blest Comforter Divine;"

Bishop George W. Doane:
>"Softly now the light of day;"

George W. Bethune:
>"When time seems short and death is near;"

William A. Muhlenberg:
>"I would not live alway;"

Samuel F. Smith:

    "The morning light is breaking;"

and

    "My country, 'tis of thee;"

William C. Bryant:

    "When the blind suppliant in the way;"

and

    "Deem not that they are blest alone;"

and

    "O Thou, whose own vast temple stands;"

Oliver Wendell Holmes:

    "Lord of all being, throned afar;"

and

    "O Love divine, that stooped to share;"

John G. Whittier:

    "It may not be our lot to wield;"

and

    "We may not climb the heavenly steeps;"

Mrs. Elizabeth P. Prentiss:

    "More love to thee, O Christ;"

and Ray Palmer:

    "My faith looks up to Thee."

Chapter XVIII.

THE SUNDAY-SCHOOL.

1. The Religious Training of the Young in the colonial period was carefully conducted. The secular school gave special attention to the reading of the Scriptures and religious instruction. More attention was paid in the home to the religious education of the young than at any subsequent time. Schools had not multiplied, and the New England colonists were very jealous of a personal supervision of the early religious instruction of their children. The General Court of Massachusetts Colony, in 1641, made legal provision for the catechizing of the children. Scripture selections were committed to memory. Then there was an intimate acquaintance with the exact language of the Bible, which has probably never been surpassed, except in Scotland.

2. The First Attempt in America to establish the Sunday-school, with instruction by voluntary teachers, was made by the Methodists in Virginia, in 1784. This was temporary, but afterwards revived in other parts of the country. A Sunday-school Society was founded in Philadelphia, in 1790, with Bishop White, of the Protestant Episcopal Church, at the head. The special object was the instruction of the poor, but it cannot be doubted that all classes soon received the benefit of the movement. In 1823 a measure was adopted for extending the Sunday-school system in many parts of the country. Out of this effort the American Sunday-school Union was developed, which still exists, and which, by its publications and evangelistic force on the frontier, and in the neglected portions of the cities, has gathered multitudes of children within Sunday-schools.

3. **All the Churches** saw the necessity of establishing the Sunday-school and making provision for its extension. There is now no church of any numerical strength which does not have the Sunday-school, and does not regard it as an essential part of its system of aggressive work. In the cities and the sparsely settled parts of the country alike, the method has been to found a mission-school in a neglected region. Out of the school has developed the church. Many of the large and flourishing churches throughout the country have grown out of these humble beginnings, and are now sufficiently strong to organize Sunday-schools and missions themselves.

4. **The International System of Sunday-school Instruction** is a notable advance on all the previous methods of Sunday-school work. As early as 1826 the American Sunday-school Union recommended a uniform system of Sunday-school instruction; but this failed to receive the support of the general Christian public, and was abandoned. The present International system was adopted in 1873. The lessons are arranged by a committee representing the various religious bodies of the United States. Not only is the instruction thus uniform, but many of the better methods of Sunday-school work are now shared alike by all the great religious bodies. The adoption of the "International Series of Sunday-school Lessons" has been one of the strongest forces for bringing into closer fellowship all the great

ecclesiastical bodies of the United States. The working together for the spiritual building up of the young has of itself a subtle power to make men forget their points of doctrinal divergence. The Chautauqua Assembly owes its origin to the Rev. John H. Vincent, now Bishop Vincent, and the Hon. Lewis Miller. It began in 1874, and has steadily developed since then. It has its branches in various parts of the United States and foreign lands.

5. **The Sunday-school Literature** has grown to be a large and important department of our general religious literature. Its great development has been within the last three decades. The adoption of the "International Lessons" has contributed to the increase of expository books. The different churches have published their own commentaries on the lessons; while works on collateral topics, such as sacred geography, history, and archæology, have multiplied to a remarkable degree. The rich literature which the new impulse in Sunday-school teaching has produced is one of the greatest triumphs of the Church of the present century. Many of the denominational publishing houses have, each, a large Sunday-school department. Some of the best religious literature of the American Church has appeared under the name of Sunday-school publications. The American Sunday-school Union is itself a large publishing house, and has contributed to our permanent literature many of its very best works, not only by the republication of excellent foreign works, but by productions of our native authors.

Chapter XIX.

THE AMERICAN PULPIT.

1. **The Preachers of America** have not been behind their brethren of the Old World in any of the great characteristics which distinguish a capable and successful ministry. The first preachers in the colonies were men of remarkable gifts. Their education was superior, and they thought intensely. They were the real founders of the New England commonwealths. The legislation seems to have been largely directed by them. But for the inspiration which they gave to the cause of education, the great institutions of learning would never have come into existence at so early a period. Harvard College was the direct result of Shepard's preaching. Yale, Princeton, Bowdoin, and Brown are monuments to the preachers' power to establish educational advantages. Their support was often very scanty—a piece of land and a few hundred dollars. Much of the salary was often paid in produce. It was a time of "high study and low living." The young ministry in the colonial time were in the habit of getting their theological training in the homes of older pastors. Before Andover was established, it was quite common to study with the experienced pastor. Bellamy, Smalley, Hart, West, Emmons, Somers, Hooker, Charles Backus, and President Timothy Dwight were examples of the clergy who educated young men for the ministry in their own homes. Tyler educated thirty theological

students in his house in the short space of five years.

2. **The Leaders of Thought and Reform** in all our critical periods have included preachers in their number. In the War of Independence many of them were among the most powerful advocates of separation from the mother country. They aroused the people to enthusiasm amid all the sanctities of the Christian Church, and kept the people under the spell of their influence until the war was over. Without the clergy at that time the independence of the United States could not have been achieved. The same fact applies to the great Civil War of 1861–65. The churches were often the places where regiments were convened before marching southward, and where the soldiers listened to strong appeals from the pulpits to defend the national union. No army has ever been more fully supplied with chaplains than the Federal army. They shared the dangers of the field and the prison, and in some cases took the places of officers on the field of battle. In the creation of the strong sentiment for the abolition of slavery, the pulpit had its full share of work. Men forgot the errant theology of Channing and Parker and others in the might of their appeal for the universal brotherhood of man. In the promotion of revivals, the type furnished in the colonial times by Whitefield, Frelinghuysen, the Tennents, Edwards, and others have been perpetuated ever since. Nettleton, Payson, Finney, Lord, Lyman Beecher, and others have swayed multitudes by the power of their appeals to lead a Christian life, and whole churches and great organized movements have grown out of them. Moody, without the formality of clerical orders, has been a mighty preacher of the Word for twenty years. Har-

rison, Small, and others have done great service in gathering in the multitudes. Cable, the *littérateur*, is teaching thousands the way of life by his Bible instruction.

3. **Homiletical Literature.**—Among the most numerous publications of the early American press were sermons. A great many of Cotton Mather's three hundred and eighty-eight publications were single sermons, and the same holds true of many of his contemporaries and successors. The sermon, often as elaborate as though written by the logical Barrows, might fitly be called a theological treatise. It soon found its way into print. The clerical wisdom of first producing in the pulpit, and then giving the sermon to the larger public, was an early gift of the Puritan settlers. As the press had much to do with the birth of Puritanism, so it was liberally used to sustain and propagate it. The sermon in print was highly appreciated in all the great crises of the earlier American history. Franklin regarded it as a good investment to print the sermons of Whitefield, William Tennent, and others. President Dwight published his theological system in the form of sermons, in four octavo volumes. The most influential of all printed sermons in America have not been produced here, but are the work of Frederick W. Robertson, of Brighton, England. Among the most notable of American preachers who have recently passed away are Bushnell, Simpson, William Adams, and Henry Ward Beecher. Among living preachers may be mentioned Richard S. Storrs, Phillips Brooks, Theodore L. Cuyler, T. DeWitt Talmage, Parkhurst, G. Dana Boardman, Charles F. Deems, J. A. Broadus, John P. Newman, Charles H. Fowler, and David Swing.

Chapter XX.

THEOLOGY OF THE AMERICAN CHURCH.

1. **The Early American Theology** was serious and fundamental. The doctrinal differences of the Old World had caused the Puritan emigration. The thinking revolved about the foundations of Christianity. Never was so much theological meditation, fortified by appropriate Scripture proofs, produced amid such humble surroundings as in our early New England colonies. The echoes from the Westminster Assembly were heard throughout New England, and produced their effect in the log-house of the humblest colony. Theological terms were well understood, and the finer points had their discriminating judges in men clad in homespun.

2. **The Scriptural Period** was the first stage in our theology. The Bible was uppermost in every mind. A doctrinal tenet which was purely speculative, and had no direct Scriptural proof, passed as of little value. The Westminster Catechism, the Savoy Confession, and the Thirty-nine Articles of the Church of England were the universal bases of belief. These were claimed to be derived directly from the Bible, and stood next to it in the love of the people. The Scriptures were read daily in the domestic circle, and often the head of the family used the original Hebrew and Greek. Scriptural themes were frequent in academic use. Cotton Mather's address, on taking

his degree as Bachelor of Arts, was based on "The Divinity of the Hebrew Points." "We record," says an author, "at our country's origin a favorable impulse to the employment of our native good sense in theological investigation; for our fathers made an open renunciation of all prescriptive systems, and took the Bible alone for their text-book."

3. **The Liberalizing Period** came as a result of the introduction of the Half-way Covenant. Many persons coming into the Church without profession of regeneration, a large amount of loose theology came in with them. Less attention was given to the confessions. The Bible was regarded as of less importance than in the earlier time. Many people looked upon the severer thinking of their fathers as good enough for the beginning of colonial life, but not suited to the more advanced period. The reaction against the Scriptural letter opened wide the door for a too liberal theological tendency. The result was the Unitarian revolt.

4. **The Controversial Period** was the next stage in our theology. While the great revival at the middle of the eighteenth century did much to restore the old theological firmness, the tendency now was to a discussion of great Scriptural themes. Jonathan Edwards, of Northampton, by his work on "The Freedom of the Will," opened the door to a line of controversy which has broken out afresh, at intervals, ever since. His work was the best philosophical structure ever reared on the Calvinistic theology, whether in the Old World or the New. The Congregationalists were most affected by this controversy. While the Presbyterians were agitated by the discussion, they were never diverted from a line which they early chose—the literary qualifications of their ministry, a thorough Chris-

tian experience, and a zeal in occupying new territory. The favorite theological text-books of the pre-revolutionary period had been Ames's "Medulla," Wolleb's "Compendium," and Willard's "Body of Divinity." But some other works came in to take their place. The writings of Edwards, who is the real founder of "New England Theology," took the place of these primitive works. The three authors who built on the Edwardean foundation were Bellamy, in his "True Religion;" Smalley, in his "Distinction between Natural and Moral Inability;" and Hopkins, in his "Reduction of Disinterested Love to a System of Theology."

5. **The Unitarian Period** was the next in order of time. The opponents of the Trinity took their theology from the unevangelical writers of the Old World. One of the most powerful men in bringing on the Unitarian revolt was Chauncey, of Boston, who, in his "Seasonable Thoughts on the State of Religion in New England," published in 1743, took ground against the great revival. His long pastorate of sixty years was of disintegrating force, and he died an Arian. Mayhew, of the West Church, Boston, exerted a similarly evil influence in leading off many towards the Unitarian fold. The "Monthly Anthology," which was commenced in Boston in 1803, was the organ of the Unitarian philosophers. Moses Stuart and Leonard Woods were among the leaders of the evangelical opposition to the rising Unitarianism.

6. **The Hopkinsian Theology** was a toning down of the strict Calvinism of Edwards and his school. The leaders were Hopkins, Bellamy, the younger Edwards, West, Spring, and Emmons. They differed from the elder Calvinism as to the nature of human depravity,

the imputation of Adam's sin, the nature and extent of the atonement, and the natural inability of the unregenerate to become Christians. They were warm advocates of revivals, benevolent institutions, and missionary movements; and they founded the *Theological Magazine* (New York), the *Evangelical Magazine* (Connecticut), and the *Missionary Magazine* (Massachusetts). The strict Edwardean Calvinists and the Hopkinsians were two distinct classes at the beginning of the present century. Each operated on the other favorably. In due time they approached and amalgamated, though without any formal action. The union of the Calvinistic *Panoplist* with the Hopkinsian *Missionary Magazine*, in 1808, was one of the public evidences of the union.

7. **The Irenical Period** is the latest stage in American theology. While each of the great religious denominations has its theological system, and has developed its systematic theology from the basis of its Confession, there has been a notable absence of the polemic spirit. The Edwardean theory of the Will has been ably answered by Whedon, from an Arminian point of view, but without acrimony. The universal tendency now is, in treating doctrinal theology, not to pull down another, but to build up one's own system. Everywhere the spirit is constructive. Many of our younger theological writers have studied in German universities, and in some instances have brought over with them some views which would have been in better place if left in the Fatherland. As they advance, however, they indicate a disposition to lay aside some of the superfluities called "Higher Criticism," and to adapt themselves to the sphere of ascertained Scriptural truth.

INDEX.

Africa, the New, 110.
Alliance, the Evangelical, 105.
American Church, the missionary spirit of the, 107.
American Sunday-School Union, the; its origin and its publications, 118, 119.
Anti-Slavery Reform, the, 95–98; its advocates, 96–98.
Awakening, the great, in the Northern colonies, not felt so much in the Southern colonies, 47, 48.

Baltimore, Lord, first and second, 17.
Baptists, the: lead in inaugurating voluntary church support, 65, 66; their work of evangelization, 70; their founding, spread, zeal, and culture, and their smaller sects, 74, 79: the Free (Will), 79.
"Bay Psalm Book," the, 50.
Berkeley's, Sir William, opposition to schools in the colonies, 36, 37.
Bible Society, the American, founding of, 68.
Book of Mormon, origin of, 92, 93.
Brainerd's, David, work among the Indians, 56.

Cambridge Platform, the, 32.
Carolinas, the, a refuge, 3; colonized from Virginia, 18.
Carroll, John, 83.
Cavaliers, the, 2, 3, 13.
Channing, William Ellery, 87.
Chautauqua Assembly, the, 119.
Christendom, the New, 1–3.
Christians, the, threefold origin of, 90, 91.
Church, the, at the founding of the Republic, 62–64; numerical strength of, at the beginning of the National Period, 64; a part of the colonial system, 65.
——— government in the colonies, 31–34.
——— of England, the, 29, 31, 72.
——— the German Reformed: its origin, members, territory, and clergy, 75.
——— the Lutheran: its origin, leaders, territory, schools, and theology, 75, 76.
——— the Methodist Episcopal: its beginnings, leaders, first Conference, division, Centennial and Œcumenical Council, 77; its smaller bodies, 79, 80; favors temperance, 100.

128　INDEX.

Church, the Moravian: its origin, territory, missionary zeal, and schools, 76, 77.
—— the Presbyterian: its origin, first General Assembly, division into New and Old School, reunion, culture, zeal, and theology, 76; its subdivisions, 78; Reformed, 78; Cumberland, 79; favors temperance, 100.
—— the Protestant Episcopal: work of, for the Indians, 55, 56; growth in Southwest, 71; its founding, growth, and characteristics, 72, 73; first General Convention of, 72.
—— the Reformed, 30, 44; effort for the Indians, 55; its founding, 73; secession from, of the True Reformed Church, 74; its theology and clergy, 74.
—— the Roman Catholic, 82–84; its colonial missions, a failure, 82; its care for its immigration, a success, 82, 83; its numbers—a shrinkage, 82, 83; its organization and educational system, 83.
—— and State, separation of, 65, 66.
—— the Unitarian: its origin, leaders, and literary spirit, 85, 86.
Club, the Transcendental, of Boston, 87.
Colleges, affected by the revival of 1797, 67, 68; a result of preachers' labors, 120.
Colonization Society, the American, 97.
Columbus: his religious faith, and the effect of his discovery, 4.
Commission, the Christian, 106; the Sanitary, 106.
Congregationalists, the: the descent, clergy, theology, literary fertility, and educational enterprise, 73; Unitarians sprung from, 85.
Congress, the First, resolution of, against distilling liquors, 99.
Continental Colonies, the, 21–24.
Controversial period, the, of American theology, 124.
Controversies in Old and New World contrasted, 62, 63.
Coöperation, Christian, 106.
Cortes conquers Mexico, 4, 5.
Cotton, John, 55, 58, 59, 73; Catechism of Richard Mather and, 111, 112.

Dartmouth College, grows out of an Indian school, 53.
Decline, the spiritual, at Revolutionary period, 63.
Denominations, the leading evangelistic, 70; the larger and earlier, 72–77; the smaller, 78–80; the multiplication of, 78.
Disciples of Christ, the, 79.
Dunster, Henry, 37.
Dutch, the, 21, 22.

Edmunds Law, the, 94.
Education, 35–39; the educational spirit of the first colonists, 35; elementary, 35, 36; colleges founded, 37, 38; prominent in New England and Virginia, 36–38; in Southern colonies largely private, 38, 39; gifts for, 103; of the Freedmen, 103.
Edwards's, Jonathan, "The Freedom of the Will," 124.
Eliot, John: his studies, labors, and literary work, 53–55; memorial against slavery, 95.

INDEX.   129

Emancipation, Act of, 98.
Emerson, Ralph Waldo, his position, descent, and spirit, 88.
English, the: their colonization, 12-20; their discoverers, 12.
Europe, religious and political convulsions of, during the sixteenth century, 1, 2.
Evangelical Association, the, 80.
Evangelical Magazine, the Connecticut, 113, 114, 126.
Evangelization stimulated by the revival of 1797-1803, 68.
Expansion in the South and West, 69-71.

Florida, conquest of, 5.
France looking westward, 8.
Freedmen, the present condition of the, and their children, 98; education of, 103, 104.
French, the: their colonization, 8-11; the outcome, 11; their navigators, 8, 9; along the Great Lakes, 9; collision with, and conquest by, the English in Canada, 11, 26, 27.

Georgia, an asylum, 3, 18.
Germans, the: in Pennsylvania, 23, 24; driven from the Palatinate, 23.
Grotius's "The Truth of the Christian Religion," 21.

Half-way Covenant, the, 59, 60; its effect, 60, 124.
Hanover, Presbytery of, remonstrance of, against a general assessment, 66.
Harvard College, 37; special work at, for Indians, 52; comes under control of the Unitarians, 87.
Henrico, University of, first important school in Virginia, 36.
Hopkinsianism, its leaders, doctrines, organs, and influence, 125, 126
Huguenots, the, 3, 5, 22, 23.
Hutchinson, Ann, her views, their rapid spread and decline, 58, 59
Hutchinsonian Controversy, the, 57, 58.
Hymnology, Christian, 114-116,
Hymns, twenty-five notable, by nineteen authors, 114-116.

Independence, the spirit of, invades the churches, 64.
Indians, the: visited and converted by the Jesuits, 10; their relations with William Penn, 18, 19; with the Dutch, 21; missions to, 52-56, 68, 76, 107, 108; Eliot's Bible for, 54, 111; treatment of, by the United States, 104; books for, 108.
Intemperance during the Colonial Period, 99.
International Series of Sunday-School Lessons, 118, 119.
Intolerance in the colonies, 40-45.
Irenical period, the, of American theology, 126.

James I. drives out the Pilgrims, 2.
James River Colony, the, 13.
Jefferson, Thomas, introduces an act "for establishing religious freedom," 66.
Jesuits, the: their missionaries, 9, 10, 83; their "Relations," 10; influence over the Indians, 10:

9

Lee, Ann, 90.
Liberalizing period, the, of American theology, 124.
License, high, a delusion, 102.
Literature, Christian, 111-116; of the Sunday-school, 119; homiletical, 122.
Livingston, J. H., 74.
Lord's Supper, the, a new view of, 60.

Maryland, the colony of, 17, 44.
Massachusetts Bay, the colony of, 14, 15.
Mather, Cotton, 61, 73, 123, 124.
—— Increase, 61, 73.
Methodists, the: their work of evangelization, 70, 71; first Sunday-school, 117.
Mexico, conquest and conversion of, 4, 5.
Millerite movement, the, 91.
Missionary Magazine, the Massachusetts, 114, 126.
Missions, 107-110; to the Mormons, 94; Home, 108, 109; Foreign, five great fields, 109; organization of societies, 108, 109.
Mississippi Valley, the, 9, 10, 26, 69.
Molina's Aztec and Spanish Dictionary, 7.
"Monthly Anthology," 125.
Moravians, the, 19, 20.
Mormon abomination, the, its antecedents, book, growth, and antidote, 92-94.

New England, church laws in, 31; intolerance in, 40-43; preachers of, able political guides, 46, 47; "Primer," 111, 112.
New Sweden, colony of, 22.

Oglethorpe, 18, 20.
Option, local, 102.

Panoplist, the, 114, 126.
Parker, Theodore, 87, 88.
Penn, William, 18, 19, 81.
Periodical religious press, the, 113, 114.
Philanthropy and Christian Union, 103-106.
Pilgrims, the, 2, 14.
Plymouth Colony, the, 13, 14; amalgamation of, with Massachusetts Bay, 16.
Political framework of the colonies, 28-30; four varieties of authority, 28, 29.
Prayers, long, in Puritan service, 49, 50.
Preachers, the, of America, 120, 122.
Presbyterians, the, in Virginia, 44; their work of evangelization, 70.
Prince's, Thomas, "Christian History," 113.
Prohibition, constitutional, 101.
Protestantism: how affected by the conquest of the French in Canada, 11, 26, 27; rapid growth of, in Maryland, 17, 18; vigor of, 25, 26.
Protestants, the: the current westward, 69, 70; Poles and Italians, 20.
Providential planting, the, 25-27.

"Psalterium Americanum," the, 50, 112.
Pulpit, the American, 120-122.
Puritans, the, 15, 16, 40; writings of, 48; theologians, 57.

Quakers, the, 19; persecution of, 41; co-operate with Presbyterians for religious freedom, 66; origin and leaders, 81; Hicksite, 91; protest against slavery, 95, 96; favor temperance, 99.

Recorder, the Boston, the first religious weekly, 114.
Reform, preachers as leaders of thought and, 121.
Reforming Synod, the, 32, 33.
Religious liberty, diversity of, among the colonies, 30; an act for establishing, in Virginia, 66.
Religious life, the, of the colonies, 46-48.
Religious motive, the, supreme with colonists, 2, 3, 46.
Revival, the, of 1797-1803, 67, 68; advantages of, 67, 68.
Revolution, the close of, a critical time for the Church, 63.
Rhode Island, 42, 74.
Robert College, 109.
Robinson, John, 14, 52.
Roman Catholics: first on the field, 4; missionaries in Mexico, 5; publications of, in Spanish, 6, 7; in Maryland, 17, 44; grounds of opposition to, 44, 45; in the West and South, 69; and the public schools, 84; their parochial schools, 84.
Rush's, Dr., "The Effects of Ardent Spirits," etc., 100.

Saloon, the friends of the, 101, 102.
Salzburgers, the, 20.
Saybrook Platform, the, 34.
Sceptical tendencies from France, 63.
Scotch-Irish, the, 19, 76; driven to America, 19; revival among, 67.
Scriptural period, the, of American theology, 123.
Sermon, the, the chief part of Puritan service, 49; the printed, as a form of literature, 122.
Shakers, the, 90.
Significance, the moral, of the Protestant occupation of the West and South, 71.
Slavery, American, the outgrowth of European cupidity, 95; protest against, from colonies, 95, 96; opposition to, at Revolutionary period, 96; the quiescent period, 97.
Smith, Joseph, 92.
Spanish, the: their colonization, 4-7; their greed and cruelty, 5, 6; evils of, in Mexico and other colonies, 5, 6.
Sunday-school, the, 117-119.
Swedenborgians, the, their organization, General Convention, and territory, 89, 90.
Swedes, the, 22; conflict of, with the Dutch, 22.
Synods, the, of New England, 31, 32.

Temperance Reform, the, in first Congress, 1774; early leaders in, organizations, constitutional prohibition, 99-102.
Territorial distribution providential, 26, 27.
Texas, 5, 27.
Thanksgiving and fast-day services, 50, 51.
Theological movements, 57-61.
Theology of the American Church, 123-126.
Transcendentalists, the, 87, 88.
Transferal of European conflicts to America, 2.

Union, Christian, 105.
Unitarian period of American theology, 125.
Unitarians, the: their origin, 61, 85; philanthropy and culture, 87; the effect of the Half-way Covenant, 124.
United Brethren in Christ, the, 79.
Universalists, the, and other smaller bodies, 89-91.

Virginia, first charter of, 2, 3; ecclesiastical rival of Plymouth, 40; intolerance in, 43, 44; first to adopt the voluntary principle, 65.

Ware, Dr., election of, to professorship in Harvard, 85.
Washingtonian movement, the, 100.
West, the, the churches of, their wonderful growth and vigor, 71.
Western Reserve, the, 70.
Whedon's answer to Edwards on "The Freedom of the Will," 126.
Wheelock's, Eleazar, school for the Indians, 52, 53.
Wheelwright's connection with Hutchinsonianism, 57-59.
Whitefield, George, 47.
"Whole Book of Psalms," the, 112, 113.
Willard's, Samuel, lectures on the Shorter Catechism, 113; his "Body of Divinity," 125.
William and Mary College, 87, 38.
Williams, Roger, 30; his expulsion from Salem, 42, 43; real ground of his banishment, 43; founder of Baptist Church in America, 74.
Woman's Christian Temperance Union, 101.
Worship and usages, in the colonies, 49-51.

Young, the religious training of the, 117.
Young, Brigham, 92.
Young Men's Christian Association, 105.

Zinzendorf, Count, 76.

THE END.

www.ingramcontent.com/pod-product-compliance
Lightning Source LLC
Chambersburg PA
CBHW021936160426
43195CB00011B/1108